RESTON TOWN CENTER

RESTON TOWN CENTER

A DOWNTOWN FOR THE 21st CENTURY

ALAN WARD, EDITOR

THOMAS J. D'ALESANDRO IV

CHARLES C. BOHL

ROBERT C. KETTLER

PHILIP LANGDON

RAYMOND A. RITCHEY

ROBERT E. SIMON

ROBERT A. M. STERN

TOM VANDERBILT

new color photography by

BRYAN BECKER

ACADEMY PRESS
WASHINGTON, DC
2006

THE BOOK IS MADE POSSIBLE BY ROBERT C. KETTLER AND KSI SERVICES, INC.

ACADEMY PRESS
1657 THIRTY-FIRST STREET, NW
WASHINGTON, DC 20007
202.338.5535
WWW.ACADEMYPRESSBOOKS.COM

JAN CIGLIANO, PUBLISHER
SARA E. STEMEN, BOOK DESIGNER
JANE SHEINMAN, MAPMAKER
LUIGI PALMERI, INDEXER
LAURA LONDON, KSI SERVICES, INC., PROJECT MANAGER

PRINTED IN CHINA THROUGH ASIA PACIFIC OFFSET

CATALOGING-IN-PUBLICATION DATA ON FILE WITH THE LIBRARY OF CONGRESS
ISBN 0-9728575-1-6

TITLE PAGE: MERCURY, FOUNTAIN SQUARE.

CONTENTS

1   Sponsor's Statement

4   Introduction *A Downtown for the 21st Century*
    CHARLES C. BOHL

28 *Certainty to Flexibility: Planning and Design History, 1963–2005*
    ALAN WARD

74 *Developing Reston Town Center*
    THOMAS J. D'ALESANDRO IV

106 *Building an Urban Neighborhood*
    ROBERT C. KETTLER

122 *Visions for Reston Town Center: A Dialogue*
    ROBERT E. SIMON, RAYMOND A. RITCHEY, *and* ROBERT C. KETTLER
    with ALAN WARD

138 *Urban Tastes and Suburban Living: America's Town Centers*
    PHILIP LANGDON

156 *A Brooklyn Boy in Reston Town Center: There Should be More Places Like This*
    TOM VANDERBILT

170   *Designing the Suburban City*
ROBERT A. M. STERN

178   *Toward an Organic Model for Cities: Design Principles for a New Downtown*
ALAN WARD

189   Chronology
193   Bibliography
196   Endnotes
197   Reston Town Center Buildings
199   Acknowledgments
201   Contributors
205   Index

ICE SKATING PAVILION, FOUNTAIN SQUARE.

SPONSOR'S STATEMENT

THIS EXTRAORDINARY PRESENTATION of the Reston Town Center story highlights the achievements of visionaries Robert E. Simon, James Cleveland, Kenneth Himmel, Thomas J. D'Alesandro IV, and others, who created Reston Town Center. The talented designers RTKL Associates, Sasaki Associates, Lessard Group Architects, The Smith Group, and Robert A. M. Stern have placed the town center in the forefront of urbanism while creating buildings, landscapes, and streetscapes for people—to gather, stroll, dine, recreate, relax, window shop, people watch, and more.

In all that Reston Town Center has become—a corporate office and hotel destination, a vibrant shopping district, a lively restaurant and entertainment venue, and a dense residential neighborhood—it is a place for people. It has the feel we want from our cities. It is a place of activity as well as repose. It offers instant access to the global market in the midst of a lively town square and tree-lined streets. It is a secure and comfortable community where good will is not a stranger.

Buildings line the sidewalks. Streetfronts and shopfronts welcome and invite. Life at Reston Town Center builds on itself, attracting more life. Around Fountain Square and Freedom Square, Reston Park and Reston Town Square, along the sidewalk and shopfronts, and in the pavilion and skating rink, Reston Town Center is an attractive and convenient place for people to live, work, play, shop, meet one another, sit quietly, or just enjoy the scene.

Reston Town Center is the urban core of those who work and live nearby. One senses a dynamic urban culture. The new generation of dramatic high-rise residences and

MARKET STREET AND MULTIPLEX THEATER.

offices are promising to transform the town center into an even more vibrant 24-hour neighborhood. Those who are choosing this urban lifestyle in Reston Town Center are redefining suburban living by creating a traditional town center where they live and work. It is a downtown for the twenty-first century.

Future downtowns will emerge out of our existing suburban neighborhoods, places where the infrastructure of jobs, schools, roads, transit, stores, and civic institutions is in place. We are witnessing the urbanization of the suburbs. Reston Town Center is a model for the future.

We offer our sincere thanks to editor Alan Ward, contributors Charles C. Bohl, Thomas J. D'Alesandro IV, Philip Langdon, Raymond A. Ritchey, Robert E. Simon, Robert A. M. Stern, and Tom Vanderbilt. We are pleased our support enables Academy Press to publish this book on the remarkable and ever-evolving Reston Town Center.

Robert C. Kettler
Chairman, KSI Services, Inc.

A DOWNTOWN
FOR THE 21st CENTURY

CHARLES C. BOHL

ALL PLACES HAVE their origins and progressions: some well known and celebrated, while most others remain forever anonymous and forgettable to all except those who live, work, or hold a financial stake in them. It is disheartening to realize the development potential that was squandered in the unremitting production of sprawl throughout the second half of the prior century. *Billions* of square feet in office space, *billions* more in retail space, tens of millions of homes, condominiums, and apartments, and thousands of schools, churches, libraries, museums, and town halls now diffused throughout the U. S. metropolitan landscape held the potential to create the greatest cities in the shortest time span in the history of the earth. Instead, the development pattern fueled by an era of highway building, inexpensive oil, and unprecedented wealth resulted in a net *loss* of urbanism. Not only were no new cities built, there was an erosion of existing cities. Surveying the metropolitan landscapes created since World War II, only a handful rise above the anonymous and forgettable level. Of these, one stands out as what Tom Vanderbilt describes as an "incipient city": a "hopeful idea of a city for a centerless region."

This incipient—some would say precocious—downtown has been well known and celebrated from the very beginning, not only regionally but nationally and internationally in the fields of planning, real estate development, architecture, and urban design, garnering at least two dozen awards in its first fifteen years of occupancy. Now, thanks to this book, the origins and progressions of Reston Town Center have been recorded and can be shared with this and future generations of developers, town founders, community builders, and place makers. It is a story well worth telling, both as a defining moment in twentieth-century planning and design and as an extraordinary case study in

real estate development that has begun to pull ahead of its teeming edge-city neighbors that until recently overshadowed it.

Calling Reston Town Center "a downtown for the 21st century" may strike many as hubris given its short lifespan, but when examined within its historical era and judged alongside its contemporary peers as opposed to places hundreds of years older, Reston Town Center's enormous significance as a model for new downtowns emerges. It is a project that represented a dramatic turning point in architecture and planning in the U. S. that a decade or two before had been dominated by modernist planning and design, and in the field of real estate development that was focused on the production and refinement of suburban development typologies. Reston Town Center, since planning was initiated in the mid-1960s to its build-out by 2010, would help initiate a shift from a *project* mentality, oriented towards the shorter-term production and sale of real estate *products*, to a broader enterprise carefully phased to create progressively greater value through long-term *place making*. In the process, it would redefine the nature of mixed-use development in mainstream real estate practice in the United States, and provide advocates of smart growth and new urbanism with a rare built example of a new downtown that is pedestrian-friendly, transit-ready, civic-oriented, and commercially viable.

A TALE OF TWO CENTERS

The genesis of Reston Town Center includes high drama. The first act involved a long struggle between modernism and traditional urbanism for the soul of the town center plan. The story involves a tale of two centers: Lake Anne Village Center, the modernist set piece designed by William Conklin for Robert E. Simon in the 1960s, and Reston Town Center, the downtown that eventually adopted a more traditional urban design in the 1980s. Simon's "Visions for Reston Town Center: A Dialogue," reveals his intentions with respect to the town center, and the full chronology of competing plans and schemes are described in greater detail in Alan Ward's sweeping account, "Certainty to Flexibility: Planning and Design History."

Lake Anne Village Center followed in the path of new town centers produced between 1950 and 1980 for master-planned communities and new towns. The impulse during this era was to invent a completely new type of town center for this new age. The new town centers adhered to a principle of strict separation of pedestrians and vehicles—effectively depriving the street of any civic animation and opportunity to contribute to the town center. Superblocks with minimal through-streets replaced the historic urban grid, and smaller, formal urban open spaces such as squares and village greens were eliminated in favor of vast open spaces. Retail uses were incorporated into buildings based on conventional shopping centers and malls, and gathering places would include spacious plazas bordered—but not really enclosed—by individual buildings with virtually uniform facades extending hundreds of linear feet rather than by the traditional hodgepodge of architecture and building types. In sum, modernist town centers failed to recreate the pedestrian character, human scale, commercial dynamics, and intimate public spaces of historic centers.

Lake Anne Village Center is one of the most innovative efforts from this era. The center avoided the megastructure excess of its contemporaries across Europe and Scandinavia that assembled all of a town center's uses under a single roof. It also incorporated many ideas shunned in other new towns, including vertically mixed uses (residences over shops), and a partially enclosed piazza that opens onto Lake Anne. Although there are no streets and the modernist architecture is austere, Lake Anne Village Center has attracted and maintained a loyal base of residents and "live-work" pioneers long before the terminology had come back into fashion.

Reston Town Center's gradual shift away from early proposals characterized by modernist planning approaches and towards the more traditional urban design chronicled the demise of experimental town center formats. Each revision to the town center's master plan since the early 1960s revealed a renewed appreciation of the age-old wisdom embodied in main streets, walkable blocks, street-oriented shop fronts, and open air streets and plazas as essential elements of a public realm and a commercially viable town center. Most importantly, whereas Simon had directed designers to create an "unexpandable" plan for Lake Anne Village Center, as Ward explains, twenty years later Reston's planners would give the town center an 85-acre core and 460-acre district in which to expand over time with built-in flexibility to respond to market conditions through a phased development strategy.

THE DIVIDING LINE FOR 20TH-CENTURY
SUBURBAN AND URBAN DEVELOPMENT

The second act of Reston Town Center's drama would concern the question of just how urban or suburban the town center would become. Surveying the plans generated up to the early 1980s, the town center appeared destined to adopt a conventional suburban vocabulary rather than an urban paradigm. These plans and renderings included what were essentially enclosed shopping malls, long, low-rise structures, vast street-free zones surrounded by surface parking, and clearly non-urban elements such as petting zoos nearby.

The turning point occurred in 1983 when a ULI plan advisory panel was asked to evaluate four proposals for the town center produced by RTKL. The panel of real estate developers might have been expected to favor lower-risk, tried-and-true, suburban development approaches found in contemporary planned communities. Instead, the entrepreneurial group expressed a collective disappointment with all the plans and posed the fundamental question concerning the town center's fate: "Is Town Center urban, or is it a high-density suburban center?" It was a watershed moment for Reston Town Center. It signaled the return of the town center in America, and established a new direction for more urban, pedestrian-friendly, mixed-use development in the United States.

Reston Town Center's dramatic shift to traditional urbanism and a downtown model would not have been nearly as significant had the project's economic and civic performance floundered. The development world had plenty of examples of exciting plans and designs that had gone bankrupt and this town center now faced the test of the marketplace.

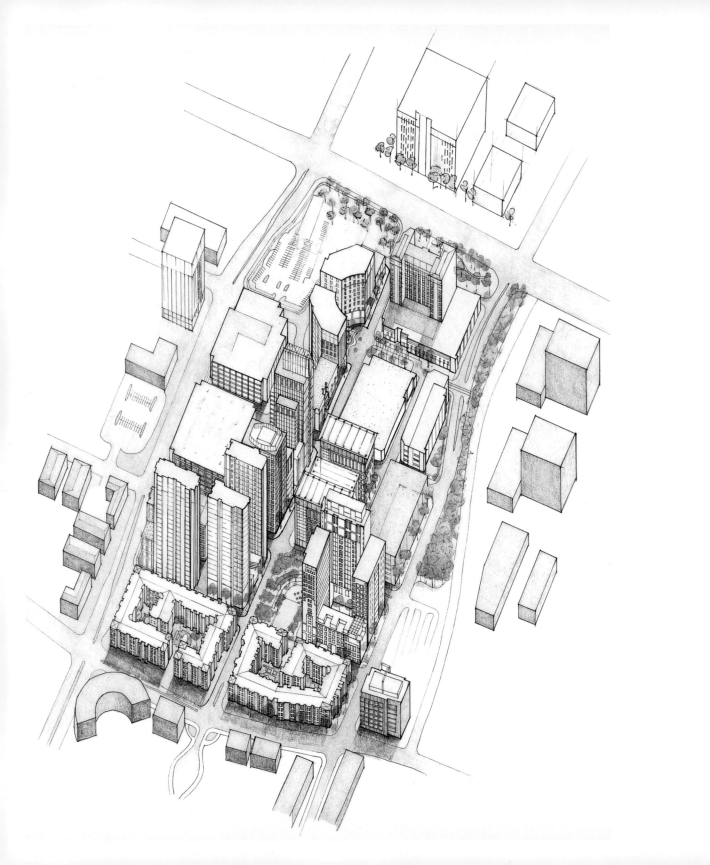

To many observers the more intensive urban build-out scenarios for the urban core and the larger town center district projected by the town center's owners, developers, and planners seemed impossibly long-term, risky propositions in the suburban market of northern Virginia in the mid-1980s, and looked like a potential disaster in 1990 when the first phase of development brought a half-million square feet of office space into a market that was in full retreat. The early success of Reston Town Center's hotel, retail, dining, and entertainment helped offset a slower lease-up of the office space, half of which remained vacant two years after the first office building was completed in 1990.[1]

The chapters by developers Thomas J. D'Alesandro IV and Robert C. Kettler tell Reston Town Center's story since the early 1990s, a story of the dynamic, market-driven build-out of the urban core and the town center district. It is a story made possible by the critical commitment of the owners and management to stay the course, staving off attempts to prematurely slice up the town center district into superblocks and develop it as conventional suburban pods of single-use developments. D'Alesandro credits the fact that many of the early Reston team remained involved with the successive ownership and developers, and that many of these team members lived and worked in Reston. Key actors like D'Alesandro viewed Reston Town Center's development from both a real estate and a community building perspective, with an appreciation of the original vision, a pragmatic approach for phased development, and a long-term perspective for the ultimate build-out potential.

The completion of the town center is now moving at a breathtaking pace with a mix of residential, office, and retail development, the extension of the urban grid, and the addition of new gathering places. The two Freedom Square towers completed in 2002 added 800,000 square feet of first-class office space and 40,000 square feet of retail in 16- and 18-story high-rise buildings, significantly taller than the original 10-story Fountain Square buildings. The town center's coming of age became palpable in 2003, when the developer Boston Properties invested a record $305 million for one of the Freedom

OPPOSITE
RESTON TOWN
CENTER
AXONOMETRIC MAP.

Square towers. Explaining why his company was so bullish, Jan Kaylor of Boston Properties highlighted the value-added of the town center setting:

> We are big believers in Reston Town Center. . . . If you look at Northern Virginia overall, there's a lot of space available. But if you look at Reston Town Center and within a quarter mile of it, you have a vacancy rate of less than 5 percent, [compared with 23 percent in the overall Reston-Herndon high-tech area]. Even in a soft market, there's a flight to quality. Tenants want to be as close as possible to amenities, the restaurants and retail.[2]

Kettler's chapter, "Building an Urban Neighborhood," recounts the long-awaited arrival of a critical mass of residential units. Housing in the town center began in earnest in 1998 with the development of West Market, a high-density neighborhood of 320 three- and four-story townhouses and condominiums located just west of the urban core. West Market's streetscapes were more urban than any other place in Reston's villages, with buildings pulled up close to the sidewalks, and trees and parallel parking lining the streets. This successful introduction of higher-density, attached housing raised developers' confidence for introducing even higher-density housing beginning in 2002 with Stratford House, a 14-story condominium building across Reston Parkway that terminates the view down Market Street, and then in 2003 the 14-story Paramount that stands across New Dominion Parkway from the town center.

In the urban core itself, Trammel Crow Residential built 700 condominiums in two, four-story buildings; the housing mixed with groundfloor retail shops at a density exceeding 80 units per acre. KSI's Midtown project will add another 1,000 units and over 40,000 square feet of retail in seven buildings ranging from two, 21-story condominium towers to a seven-story loft building. The Midtown neighborhood is built at a net density of 163 units per acre.

The value-added of the town center environment has paid off handsomely. The residential properties in the district have sold rapidly and commanded high premiums over comparable units elsewhere in the region. The high-rise, mixed-use office buildings housing the headquarters of Fortune 500 companies, such as Titan and Accenture, and the diversity of upscale, mixed-use urban housing products added in the past eight years would have been unthinkable without the foundation of the urban master plan and the down-town core established in the first phase. The amenities of attractive urban streets, outdoor dining, shops, entertainment, and animated public spaces that include the glass-canopied skating rink and Fountain Square's cascading Mercury fountain, all within easy walking distance of homes and offices are now cited as a decisive factor in the success of Reston Town Center. They deliver the intangible qualities associated with a more cosmopolitan lifestyle highlighted in Philip Langdon's "Urban Tastes and Suburban Living" and Tom Vanderbilt's "A Brooklyn Boy in Reston Town Center: There Should Be More Places Like This."

Vince Graham, the developer of the traditional neighborhood developments of Newpoint and I'On in South Carolina, describes why mixed-use communities garner more value to both their builders and residents than do single-use projects: "If what you sell is privacy and exclusivity, then every new house is a degradation of the amenity. However, if what you sell is community, then every new house is an enhancement of the asset." Reston Town Center has clearly been selling community. In contrast to its edge city competitors around the Washington region, where each additional single-use office building, shopping center, and condominium project diminishes its setting by soaking up road capacity and services without contributing public amenities, each addition to the town center has added to the urban ambience, activities, and lifestyle of the town center, the value of its real estate, and the quality of life of people who live, work, shop, and dine here.

TOP
FRIENDS MEETING
ON MARKET STREET.

BOTTOM
ART FORUM SHOP,
ONE FREEDOM
SQUARE, MARKET
STREET.

A MODEL FOR THE 21st CENTURY?
INCREMENTAL, ADAPTABLE URBANISM

In considering Reston Town Center's merits as a model for 21st-century downtowns, the record of the project as a financial success has now been established. Its performance was consistently better than competing properties in the region through the early economic downturn of the 1990s and the freefall of the technology industry following the dot.com bust and the 9/11 attacks in 2001. The town center's property values have soared, office and residential space rents and sells at a premium, and the retail, dining, and entertainment components are all outperforming their regional competition and exceeding the average national sales figures for their sectors.

Beyond its profitability, however, an important question is the town center's value relative to the broader measures of success as a developing downtown that contributes to the social and civic needs of the surrounding community—principles that define smart growth and new urbanism. In terms of smart growth, the town center satisfies a number of principles by design: high density; compact; mixed-use; transit-oriented (with frequent bus service from the start and a Metrorail connection planned); an interconnected street grid; and parks and open space adjacent to the downtown.

The shared parking arrangement developed early on would eventually reduce the initial parking requirements by nearly 25 percent, and the gradual conversion of surface lots into urban blocks with structured parking is a model for market-driven phasing. A traffic study carried out by Wells & Associates in 2000 found that Reston Town Center generated nearly 50 percent less traffic than a comparably-sized suburban development.[3]

Fairfax County also contributed to Reston Town Center's smart growth dimensions by adopting the flexible parameters of the "Residential Planned Community–Town Center Zone." This zoning would maintain extraordinary flexibility and protection from suburban standards for building disposition, floor-area-ratios, street standards, and single-use clustering that have so often diluted and ultimately defeated attempts to create town centers.

D'Alesandro also notes the key role Fairfax County played in supporting the town center by imposing zoning restrictions on retail properties within an eight-mile radius, effectively limiting the competition during its early years and allowing the town center to blossom.

Reston Town Center's biggest achievement has been in creating a sense of place, a true gathering place with a strong identity. While the architecture might not attain Simon's vision for a more eclectic mix of smaller buildings designed by several architects, the town center manages to avoid the extremes of both modernism and the historicist appearance of other town center projects while delivering solid urban buildings that frame the streets and create good pedestrian frontages in the downtown. As Langdon notes, the architectural style is designed to convey "serious workplaces for a corporate age." It was and is architecture of both urban ambition and stylistic restraint, which has been undeniably successful in attracting major corporations to leave traffic-jammed suburban office campuses and move to Reston's mixed-use, high-rise downtown.

Housing

Reston Town Center is not perfect, however, and there is room to continue refining the town center that by historical standards is still young. The lack of affordable or moderate-income housing seems particularly unfortunate given the tremendous value created in the town center above and beyond anyone's

expectations. As Michelle Krocker, the director of housing at Reston Interfaith, observed: "There are hundreds of units going up at Reston Town Center and none are affordable."[4] The challenge to build affordable and workforce housing, however, is not unique here; it is a nationwide issue that has become more difficult with the extraordinary rise in land values and housing prices over the past decade.

The cost of housing in this and other town centers is a function of land and development costs and economics 101: supply and demand. The demand for housing in new town centers continues to exceed supply, whether it be apartments above retail in Miami Lakes Town Center in Florida and Mashpee Commons in Mashpee, Massachusetts; live-work units in Kentlands, Maryland, and Baldwin Park in Orlando, Florida; main street lofts in Reston Town Center and Orenco Station Town Center in suburban Portland, Oregon; or townhouses and mid- to high-rise condominiums in Mizner Park in Boca Raton, Florida, and Reston Town Center. Town center housing offers a way of life

WEST MARKET
TOWNHOUSES AND
CONDOMINIUMS,
WEST OF RESTON
TOWN CENTER
URBAN CORE.

that people in increasingly congested metropolitan regions want: the convenience of living, working, conducting business, socializing, and recreating without the need to drive and the ambience of an attractive urban setting. Town centers and main streets offer something that cannot be found in most suburban communities: a room with a view. By the same token, apartments and condominiums overlooking public plazas, fountains, and parks, and lofts and rowhouses looking out onto main streets are something very hard to come by outside of major cities. In lieu of policies and incentives to encourage affordable and workforce housing in town centers, the only way it might become more affordable will be to increase the supply.

Reston Town Center's housing prices also reflect market conditions within a relatively brief time, with all the units built since 1998, a period of dramatically rising prices for land and property. While Reston Town Center boasted an enviable mix of commercial office, retail, hotel, dining, and entertainment from the outset, one real estate expert of urban housing projects, Todd Zimmerman, strongly recommends that multifamily housing be included at the beginning of a town center's development.

Housing provides a hedge against downturns in commercial real estate—the office market downturn after 9/11, for example, delayed plans for office towers in West Palm Beach's City Place while accelerating a variety of town-center residential units in hot demand as investors moved money out of the stock market and into real estate—and also establishes a human presence and baseline of daily activity on the street that activates the town center outside of office and store hours of operation. Although residential prices have appreciated steadily, had units been built in Reston Town Center in 1990, when land prices were lower and market conditions very different, they would undoubtedly offer a different price point in the mix of housing today.

Streetfront Design

The town center's multi-level parking garages on the north were designed without streetfront shops, offices, or residences, an approach that is now common in town center projects and extends the walkable urban fabric beyond a single thread of a main street and into a downtown grid. In Reston Town Center, the "unfinished" garages create unfortunate dead zones immediately adjacent to the urban core, a condition that no doubt will be remedied when these blocks are redeveloped in the future to higher densities with underground parking and street-grade shops and services. The more recently constructed five-level garage on the south at Library Street and Bluemont Way shows how the inclusion of groundfloor retail can successfully reclaim the street as an attractive pedestrian realm.

The primary town center streets feature pleasant pedestrian-oriented designs, an aesthetic that terminates at the bordering parkways, which box in the urban core with high-speed thoroughfares (Reston Parkway, Town Center Parkway, and New Dominion Parkway) impeding pedestrian movement between the downtown core and the adjacent Spectrum shopping center. In the late 1980s, owner Reston Land, architects RTKL Associates, and landscape architects Sasaki Associates attempted to buffer portions of Reston Parkway with Reston Park, a wide swath of linear green between the parkway on one side and the Hyatt Hotel on the other. The buffer also acted as a setback for the downtown and further pushed apart the commercial core and the high-density residential buildings on the west. The result diluted the urban character of the town center's east side. On the west side, buildings are brought up close to Town Center Parkway, yet the width and high-speed design of the roadway remains a potential barrier for someone to walk across to the town center.

Mobility is essential to the functioning of the downtown offices, but each of the parkways could be greatly enhanced by adopting design standards in keeping with urban boulevards and avenues—Ward Parkway in Kansas City, Monument Avenue in Richmond, and St. Charles Avenue in New Orleans are examples—capable of carrying heavy traffic while knitting the town center district closer together with the core.

Civitas and Community

The town center has succeeded in providing gathering places and walkable streets that invite community socializing and support all manner of festivals and events for the residents of Reston as well as the larger region. The town center plays host to dozens of events annually, including holiday festivals, parades, sporting events, and the popular Oktoberfest and the Greater Reston Arts Council's (GRACE's) fine arts festival, which have become community traditions. Many of the events hosted are fundraising activities that support a variety of organizations and causes, and this represents a community-building role for the town center that goes beyond its physical dimension.

Reston Town Center has been criticized by some for falling short of fulfilling all of the civic dimensions of a traditional downtown. Like many new town centers, Reston's streets and outdoor public spaces are privately owned and managed. As D'Alesandro explains in "Developing Reston Town Center," private streets offered a more controlled approach for the complexity of building a multiphased town center. Similar to other town center developers in the U. S., Reston Town Center's chose to retain ownership to uphold higher levels of maintenance and security; to permit regular street closures for public events; and to allow for narrower, more pedestrian-friendly streets, on-street parking, and urban public spaces that are not typically permitted under conventional suburban codes and regulations. Langdon's chapter suggests a way to transition the private streets and gathering places into public space through the adoption of a business improvement district capable of maintaining order and safety while delivering a genuine public realm.

In terms of civic uses, the Reston Public Library and the Reston Hospital Center, located across New Dominion Parkway within the 460-acre town center, provide two important civic resources for Reston's residents. The urban core is home to the GRACE gallery and the signature glass-roofed pavilion in Fountain Square serves as an ice skating rink during the winter months and a performing arts venue throughout the summer. Yet the larger town center lacks, as of this writing, the types of civic institutions that are

*OPPOSITE,
TOP TO BOTTOM*
RESTON PARKWAY, LOOKING WEST TOWARD RESTON TOWN CENTER.

PARKING GARAGE ON FREEDOM DRIVE.

PARKING GARAGE AT LIBRARY STREET AND BLUEMONT WAY.

FREE PARKING IN RESTON TOWN CENTER'S GARAGES.

essential elements of every downtown—religious congregations, educational centers, town halls, post offices, museums, and so forth. The Washington Council of Churches, for example, at one time proposed three church sites for the town center that would have been grouped around a common plaza with shared educational facilities.

Civic institutions are often the last pieces to fall into place for new town centers. The owner/developer can help attract civic institutions and reserve sites, but the timing for the addition of civic institutions is out of the developer's control and can involve a long timeline. Public and nonprofit organizations often require lengthy fundraising efforts, which determine the schedules for financing and building civic facilities. These schedules vary widely: the town hall in Southlake Town Square, in Southlake, Texas, opened just two years after phase one of the town center was complete, but Boca Raton Center for the Arts in Mizner Park, took a dozen years to fund and build, and

MERCURY FOUNTAIN *FOREGROUND* AND PAVILION AT FOUNTAIN SQUARE PLAZA.

the Boch Center for Performing Arts at Mashpee Commons—a project older than Reston Town Center—was on the drawing boards for almost as long.

The key, and ambition, is to reserve sites for the eventual addition of civic institutions here, thus setting the stage for filling in a final missing piece in the downtown's evolution.

A Place

As a public gathering place, Reston Town Center has clearly been embraced by residents of the area. What the town center lacks in terms of formal civic institutions it makes up for in the number and variety of public arts, social, and civic events that are hosted in the public realm of its streets, parks, and gathering places. These events draw hundreds of thousands of visitors from throughout Reston and the surrounding region each year. A recent survey found that residents and visitors view Reston Town Center as a public place, and more than 90 percent of respondents agreed that the town center was not only for the residents of Reston but also people from other communities. The survey, part of an extensive study of six town centers in the U. S., including Mizner Park; Mashpee Commons; Kentlands Market Square and Main Street; Celebration in Osceola County, Florida; and Haile Village Center in Gainesville, Florida, found that Reston Town Center's social and civic qualities were rated higher by local residents than in all other cases except Celebration's town center.[5]

For over four decades, Reston Town Center has served as a laboratory for developers, town planners, urban designers, elected officials, and others seeking potential lessons and tools for realizing their own visions for town centers and downtowns. Much of what has been created and learned is brought forth in the pages that follow. This story shows that with enough land and time, a talented development team, supportive planning tools, and some flexibility, it can happen. But it is a model that reveals the importance of incremental planning, starting with a 15-acre phase in relation to an 85-acre urban core, in relation to a larger 460-acre town center district, a 7,400-acre new community, and a 6,500-square-mile region. A downtown like Reston's becomes eminently

more viable and effective when linked to plans for major infrastructure improvements and supported by zoning that directs retail, theaters, hotels, and civic institutions to the core rather than spreading reinforcing uses along strips and interchanges in all directions.

If Reston Town Center continues to be studied and improved as a model for 21st-century downtowns there is hope for reshaping and providing meaningful centers for the hundreds of centerless suburban communities where the majority of Americans now live and work. One hopes that the era of city-free growth will end in our lifetimes and Americans will learn again to build cities that can grow, adapt, and sustain a civil society and not simply prolong the disintegration of the American community. Reston Town Center has proven that the building of new cities remains not only possible, but profitable. Let us hope that our descendants reap the rewards that its lessons can teach and that some of the development potential that will be fueled by the addition of another 60 million Americans in the next 25 years can be harnessed to set the cornerstones in place for the next generation's renditions of Charleston, Chicago, Washington, D.C., or San Francisco.

LEFT
PEOPLE MEETING
IN THE PLAZA AT
RESTON TOWN
CENTER.

RIGHT
TWO FOUNTAIN
SQUARE OFFICE
BUILDING PLAZA.

RESTON PARKWAY AND RESTON TOWN CENTER, LOOKING WEST.

CERTAINTY TO FLEXIBILITY

PLANNING AND DESIGN HISTORY, 1963–2005

ALAN WARD

RESTON TOWN CENTER is taking shape as the new downtown of northern Virginia. Building the town center is the story of private enterprise creating a downtown by design. The original plans of the early 1960s were unified architectural schemes to be built as one piece; they set the entire town center in one design at one time. In reality, in the four decades since the owners, architects, and developers created those earlier plans, the town center has evolved to become a more complex place that has been designed and built block by block across time. It is an ambitious, multi-phased program that has required adjustments in thinking, and an approach of making and interconnecting successive phases. First came the framework of urban design of streets, blocks, and open spaces. Then, within that framework, different architects designed individual buildings. And then, further change occurred within the individual blocks, especially at street level. In the future, additional change is likely with the redevelopment of the existing town center blocks and buildings, as well as land surrounding the town center.

The town center coming into being represents a series of decisions by several owners, working in tandem with planners and designers. Over several decades, with each new set of proposed plans, key questions arose: How far do you take the making of a plan; How much structure is too much; What is the balance between a framework for order and an allowance for creativity to blossom within that order? This is a summary of the individuals, the precedents that influenced their thinking, and the decisions they made, evolving from certainty to flexibility. Taken together, they determine the kind of place that Reston's downtown has become.

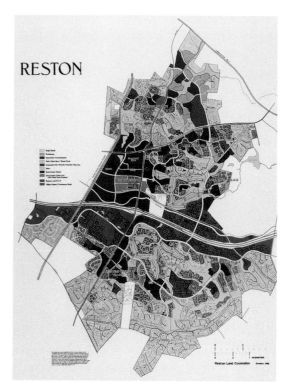

RESTON

THE VISION AND THE PRECEDENTS

As American cities and settlements have spread and grown over the continent there has been no shortage of critiques of the suburbs and sprawl. While writers, planners, and various critics of the suburbs have condemned the environment where most Americans live and work, there is also a growing number of experiments by developers and investors seeking a new model for building communities in the suburbs. Reston and its town center are part of this lineage of master-planned communities and new towns whose builders capitalized on developing land outside of central cities.

The planning for Reston began more than forty years ago, at a time of burgeoning suburbanization across America. In some respects it was part of a larger trend: since the end of World War II the growing national population expanded into areas farther from America's historic downtowns. U. S. federal policy encouraged the increase of single-family house owners, and the automobile allowed for easier transportation. Land developers and homebuilders responded to this increased demand by building housing tracts, while retail developers built shopping areas; neither usually had enough land to even consider planning an entire town. Reston was different in two important respects: Robert E. Simon had both the land and the vision.

Simon's vision for Reston was to create a new town that represented a different model for suburban development. His strategy was to concentrate development by creating urban places—a series of villages within the town, while preserving significant parts of the northern Virginia landscape. The remaining green spaces were to be laid out in corridors linking the village centers with the community's heart at Reston Town Center.

The history of American master-planned communities and new town planning that came before Reston and its town center are beyond the scope of this book. Specific precedents that bear on the direct lineage to Reston through individuals who worked on these earlier places and then later were involved in planning Reston are the most relevant. Many of the 20th-century American planned new towns had their intellectual inspiration in the garden city model put forward by Ebenezer Howard, a 19th-century English writer. Howard envisioned an alternative to the unbridled expansion of urban London by creating greenbelts within and around the center city, designed to bring people closer to the land. It was organized around a landscape that preserved the countryside in common open space, or greenbelts, with opportunities for agriculture. Concentric rings of housing and factories focused inward on a central park space designed for community gardens and a cultural center.

American architects and planners Henry Wright and Clarence Stein, who knew Howard, applied several of the garden city ideas in their 1928 plan for Radburn, New Jersey. Stein lived near Central Park West in New York City, and had been influenced by Frederick Law Olmsted's design for Central Park, notably the depressed roadways that separated vehicles and pedestrians. Stein applied Howard's ideas to Radburn by organizing lots along a framework of common, internal greenspace, a key principle of the garden city. Separating the pedestrian from the car, Stein intended this greenspace, rather than sidewalks along streets, to be the principal pedestrian route from the residential areas to the town center. Radburn's curving streets and integrated green spaces substituted for the traditional American grid pattern. Radburn became highly influential among planners, and its ideas were part of the organizing principles of the Greenbelt towns built in the 1930s by the Federal Resettlement Administration—Greenbelt, Maryland; Greenhills, Ohio; and Greendale, Wisconsin. Some of the planners and designers of these new towns would later play a prominent role in Reston Town Center.

THE NEW TOWN PLAN: 1961–1962

From an early age Robert E. Simon, Jr., had a lifelong connection to real estate. His father, Robert E. Simon, a real estate developer in New York in the 1900s, was involved in the development of Radburn. The senior Simon introduced Clarence Stein to his son, who became influenced by Stein's garden city ideas. In 1961, the younger Simon, just 47 years old, purchased 6,750 acres of land in Fairfax County, Virginia, with proceeds from the sale of Carnegie Hall in New York City. He intended to build a new community along both sides of the Dulles Toll Road, which at the time did not have an off-ramp to the property. Simon took the initials of his name, R.E.S., to name the town.

Simon had several key goals for the new town that would continue to be important through the planning process. One aim was to enable people to live and work in the same community; thus the land adjacent to the town center was reserved for commercial use. Another goal was to provide a diversity of housing types to enable an individual to live in the same neighborhood throughout his or her life and remain rooted in the community. The new town was also to provide opportunities for leisure time by offering a wide range of recreational and cultural facilities. Finally, Simon's aesthetic intentions fostered beauty in both "structural and natural" areas. To achieve these goals, Simon sought to hire what he regarded as the best planning firm in the world.

He requested proposals from several prominent firms, including Doxiados Associates from Athens, Greece, and initially settled on the St. Louis-based Harland Bartholomew and Associates, whose portfolio included new communities and retail centers, such as Westwood Village in Los Angeles. Not able to work together, however, the relationship was short-lived and Simon soon replaced Harland Bartholomew with New York-based Whittlesey & Conklin, a firm whose partners' planning experience dated to Radburn as well as the Greenbelt resettlement towns. Whittlesey & Conklin would create Reston's masterplan and lay out the first village at Lake Anne.[1]

The garden city model influenced the planning of Reston's residential villages and the preservation of significant corridors of northern Virginia woodlands between them. William Whittlesey had been on the design team for the government's Greenbelt towns; partner Albert Mayer had apprenticed with Clarence Stein during the design of Radburn. Simon presented the Whittlesey & Conklin master plan to the Fairfax County Board of Supervisors, showing clustered residential units around village centers amidst green space, as well as a high-density town center at the core. In 1962 the county approved the plan and zoned Reston a "Residential Planned Community." Reston's overall density averaged out to be comparable with conventional suburban zoning, but the concentration of residential development and higher densities in selected areas made way for significant areas of open landscape and other public spaces. This pioneering approach to town planning was later emulated across the country.

RESTON'S FIRST TOWN CENTER AT LAKE ANNE VILLAGE: 1963

Lake Anne Village was the first of Reston's five village centers. Simon recently recalled that he asked Whittlesey & Conklin to design an "unexpandable" plan for Lake Anne Village Center, intending that the village not be allowed to grow into the town center. Led by William Conklin and James Rossant, the firm also designed the plaza, the fountain, and all the village center's buildings; Washington-based architect Cloethiel Woodward Smith designed the Lake Anne townhouses. Construction began in 1963, only two years after Simon

purchased the land. For the innovative new town plan and the modernist design at Lake Anne Village, with the thirteen-story residential tower as landmark, Conklin, Rossant, and Smith were influenced by Finland's new town of Tapiola. Whittlesey and Rossant also referenced Portofino, Italy, for the plan: A south-facing crescent of buildings opened to a plaza that bordered an elongated reach of water—Lake Anne at Reston and the Mediterranean Sea at Portofino. (A south-facing crescent formed by office buildings in Reston Town Center would be developed twenty-five years later as the centerpiece of the first phase of development.)

Lake Anne Village opened in 1965 as the focus and town center of Reston for several years. It was highly acclaimed, published extensively in national and international architectural journals and popular magazines, and visited frequently by architects from around the country and abroad. Lake Anne Village Center put Reston on the design map.

LAKE ANNE
VILLAGE CENTER.

RESTON MASTER
PLAN, WHITTLESEY &
CONKLIN, 1963.

THE RESTON TOWN CENTER SITE: 1963–1964

During the same period that Whittlesey & Conklin were designing Lake Anne Village, Conklin selected the location for the future town center: a site on relatively high ground about a mile west of Lake Anne Village and less than one-half-mile north from the Dulles Toll Road. It was to be connected to the high-speed toll road by Route 602, which extended north–south and bisected the town center site. Each scheme by Whittlesey & Conklin grappled with this road—later to become Reston Parkway, the six-lane arterial divided by a median. Consistent with Radburn, Conklin separated the pedestrian from vehicular traffic.

Conklin preferred one scheme for the town center that created, in effect, a single large building with an adjoining parking structure that extended over

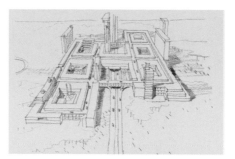

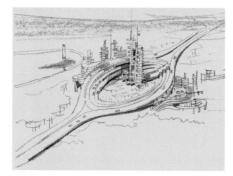

PROPOSED RESTON TOWN CENTER SCHEMES
1 *TOP LEFT*, 2 *TOP RIGHT*, 3 *MIDDLE LEFT*, AND
5 *MIDDLE RIGHT AND BOTTOM*, WHITTLESEY & CONKLIN,
1963–64.

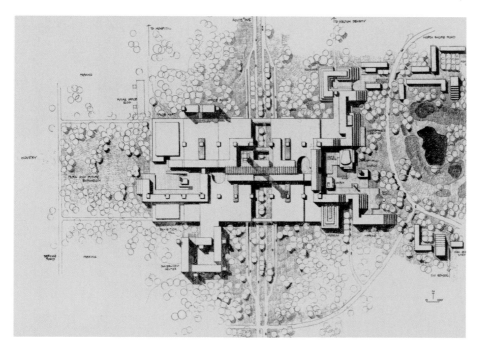

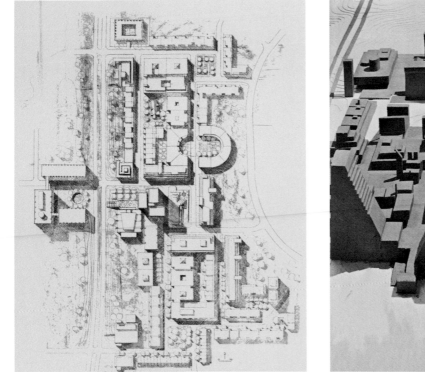

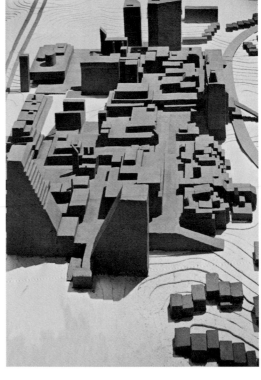

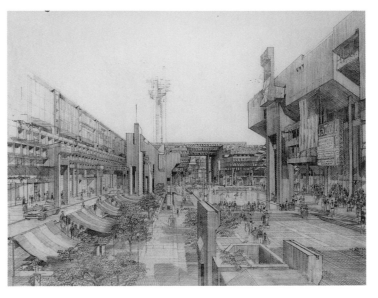

PROPOSED RESTON
TOWN CENTER
SCHEMES 7 *TOP LEFT*
AND 8 *TOP RIGHT AND*
BOTTOM, WHITTLESEY
& CONKLIN,
1963–64.

Route 602. Monumental paved plazas framed each end, surrounded primarily by eight-story buildings. Conklin recalls that he was excited by the way this scheme related to his Lake Anne Village Center design. He organized the town center buildings in a gesture resembling an open hand to the east, making connections—especially pedestrian connections—to Lake Anne Village. Conklin planned a high-density residential development, to be built in future phases along a ridge. He called this spine "an urban sinew." If this plan had been built, the town center might have grown over time into a linear pattern more than a mile long, terminating at Lake Anne Village on the east. To the west the scheme linked to a large industrial zone that extended west and south to the Dulles Toll Road.

Conklin recently described his town center scheme as a very expensive approach to building the town center. He recalls that Simon thought it was too grandiose and a challenge to build in phases. Simon noted in a June 1964 *Progressive Architecture/PA* interview that he urged the planners to step back and consider "a more modest proposal, a more conventional, small-town center where buildings are constructed individually—at ground level." Whittlesey & Conklin developed two subsequent schemes, influenced by Simon's trip to London and plans of the Bloomsbury District he sent them. *PA* apparently thought less of the Bloomsbury model than Simon, for it criticized these schemes as "conventional plans [that] swing back to commonplace planning with blocks surrounded by streets, cars, and people."

The final, preferred plan shifted the town center east of Route 602, closer to Lake Anne Village Center. The architects addressed the phasing issue by planning for future high-rise buildings on surface parking lots and replacing the parking with structures. What was remarkable about this scheme was that the lessons of the Bloomsbury District, a precinct of streets and sidewalks, seem lost. There is not a single street visible on the plan. The architects created a medieval town, with all parking below-grade. Reflecting on this in 2004, Simon recalled with some amusement that the plans were "so wonderful, they designed a town center that belongs in Rome and not in Virginia."

NEW OWNERS AND A NEW TOWN CENTER PLAN: 1967–1974

None of the Whittlesey & Conklin plans were realized. In 1967 Gulf Oil Corporation, one of the early major investors, bought out the controlling interest of Reston's real estate. Gulf unseated Simon as chairman of the board, and took over management of the planning, construction, financing, and sales of the new town. This marked the end of one individual's vision and idealism, and a transition to a more deliberate and corporate bottom-line approach— first by Gulf Reston and subsequently by Mobil Reston. It also led to new leadership, James Todd, a developer experienced with residential projects. Todd came on board as Reston's executive vice president, becoming Mobil Reston's president and chief operating officer in the decade from 1973 to 1984. In addition, the Urban Land Institute (ULI) and panels of national experts provided critical input on the strategic positioning and planning of the town center.

Gulf followed the framework of the Whittlesey & Conklin master plan for the new town generally, while bringing in new planners to study the program and plans for Reston Town Center in an effort to position the development for an improving economy. Todd hired Gladstone Associates, Washington, D.C.-based economic consultants, to analyze future development potential, and David A. Crane and Partners of Philadelphia to prepare a town center plan. The 1974 Crane plan shifted the town center site to its ultimate location today on land sloping west of Route 602 (future Reston Parkway), thereby avoiding the challenge of bridging the planned highway. (The parkway was later built as wide as eight lanes at some intersections, and four to six lanes generally.) This made links to Lake Anne Village Center impractical, but Crane and Todd, of course, did not have their predecessors' emotional attachment to Lake Anne Village Center.

Crane's objective was to test a new program; this time, phasing was a fundamental part of the planning strategy. The 1974 town center concept departed from the dense architectural compositions of the 1965 Simon era, and focused on a two-level building oriented north–south, essentially an enclosed shopping mall between two department store anchors. The plan echoed that of

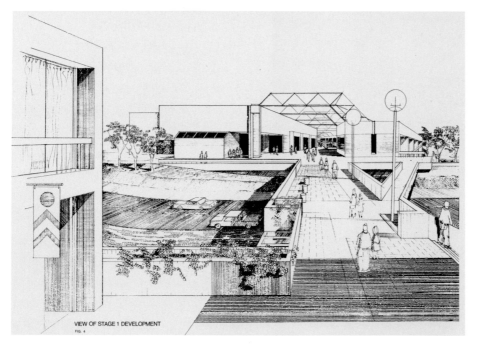

VIEW OF STAGE 1 DEVELOPMENT
FIG. 4

TOP

PROPOSED RESTON
TOWN CENTER
DEVELOPMENT PLAN,
DAVID A. CRANE AND
PARTNERS, 1974.

BOTTOM

PROPOSED PHASE I
RESTON TOWN
CENTER DEVELOP-
MENT, DAVID A.
CRANE AND
PARTNERS, 1974.

other U. S. designers' and developers' fascination with enclosed shopping environments in the early 1970s. Perhaps inspired by the arcades of Paris, the Galleria in Milan, or even the Cleveland Arcade in that city's downtown, Crane proposed "a pergola or glass roofed enclosure which would house a botanical garden on several levels," at the center of the spine, according to the 1974 report accompanying the plan.[2] A relatively fresh idea at the time, this two-level spine still projected the now all-too-familiar form of the suburban mall.

The shopping center connected on the south with a future Metrorail station—still unbuilt at this writing—that would extend to Dulles International Airport and to the north with a cluster of public buildings around a park, the "County Green." The entire plan centered on the 4,500-foot interior pedestrian spine—the length of more than ten football fields; other uses aligned with or connected to the linear city diagram. Surface parking bordered both sides while an electric mini-bus system connected with Metro at the lower mall level. The Crane approach phased the development, according to the report, with "the concept of 'densifying' the multi-use spine over time by building high rise structures on surface parking lots and replacing the parking with structures." It even introduced the idea of building over the Dulles Toll Road, to connect with the transit station. Office buildings, a sports center, and public buildings such as the library, hospital, and police station were attached to the unrelenting spine. While attempting to create a plan adaptable to changing markets and infrastructure, it is not clear that the planners actually achieved a flexible scheme.

This was the vision of Reston Town Center in 1974. With the prevailing thinking separating the automobile from pedestrians, the upper-level retail passed over the street. Unlike today's Market Street, which is a well-spaced, two-lane road lined with onstreet parking and sidewalks, the 1970s vision seemed to reflect a period of amnesia among planners and designers, this after thousands of years of making viable streets.

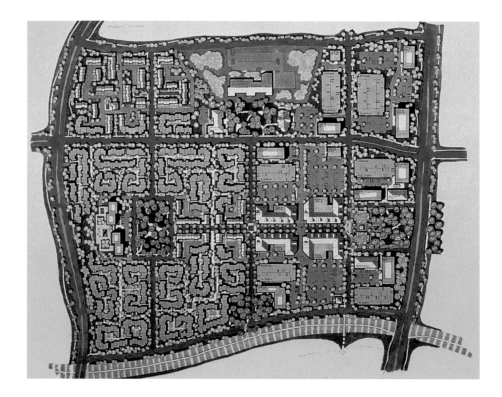

THE GRID AND A BUILDABLE
TOWN CENTER PLAN: 1978–1986

The Crane plan was never built, like the Whittlesey & Conklin plans. In 1978, Reston Land Corporation (RLC), a subsidiary of the Mobil Oil Corporation, bought out Gulf Reston's ownership when it purchased 3,700 acres of undeveloped Reston land, including the town center site. Master planning for Reston Town Center resumed in 1982 when president Jim Todd retained RTKL, a Baltimore-based architectural firm. George Pillorgè, the principal in charge, had worked on the South Lakes Village plan at Reston, and was also a project director for the "New Communities Project," a year-long study at Harvard University under architect Josep Luis Sert, funded by the U.S. Department of Housing and Urban Development. According to Pillorgè, the HUD study plan featured a dense town center, with ideas that were later incorporated into the RTKL plans for Reston Town Center.

A GRID STREET PATTERN IS INTRODUCED: RESTON TOWN CENTER SITE PLAN, MOBIL LAND AND RTKL, 1983.

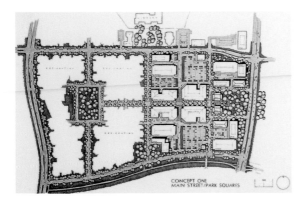

CONCEPT ONE
MAIN STREET/PARK SQUARES

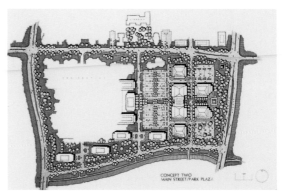

CONCEPT TWO
MAIN STREET/PARK PLAZA

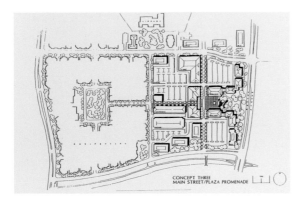

CONCEPT THREE
MAIN STREET/PLAZA PROMENADE

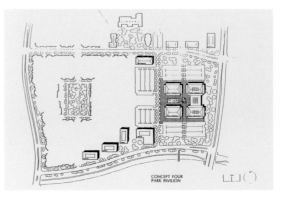

CONCEPT FOUR
PARK PAVILION

CLOCKWISE FROM TOP LEFT

CONCEPT 1, MAIN STREET/PARK SQUARES.

CONCEPT 2, MAIN STREET/PARK PLAZA.

CONCEPT 3, PARK PAVILION.

CONCEPT 4, MAIN STREET/PLAZA PROMENADE.

In each alternative, RTKL returned the town center's orientation from a north–south to an east–west axis, as originally conceived. This restored the primary connection to Reston Parkway and opened large parcels to the west for future residential development on Market Street. The four RTKL plans represented a place more limited and scaled-back than contemporary ideas about a downtown. Given perceived market demand, the densities were still quite low, with predominantly surface parking and small garages in some plans. An important element was the emerging grid pattern for retail and office uses, and a series of streets starting to break down the site into parcels. The structure of the street pattern that was ultimately built in the 1990s was partially visible in each of the plans, although the blocks were super-sized, in contrast to that which was ultimately built. Two ideas featured in these alternatives would be key to the town center ten years later: one concept was a central "main street," named Market Street, running east to west; the second was an allowance for green space, a park along Reston Parkway.

RTKL's idea of Market Street as an organizing element became even more powerful in subsequent versions of the plan. The revival of the street as the locus of activity was informed by the work of William Whyte, Jane Jacobs, and others, who had argued forcibly for sustaining the life of cities on streets and sidewalks, based on their observations of American cities. The park along Reston Parkway fulfilled certain urban planning ideals: to create a green front door to the town center; to preserve existing trees; and to create an effective setback from the traffic of what would ultimately become a six-lane parkway. However, the park and roadway created a significant break in the continuity of the town center that earlier schemes by Whittlesey & Conklin had tried to overcome by bridging over the highway. Today, the twelve-story Stratford House condominium on the east side of Reston Parkway, built on land technically part of Reston Town Center, appears disconnected from the pedestrian urban core.

Jim Todd sought input from outside professionals that were not closely involved in the project. He submitted RTKL's four alternative town center

MASTER-PLAN
ILLUSTRATIVE SITE PLAN

RTKL RESPONDED TO
ULI CRITIQUE AND
CONVERTED DEVEL-
OPMENT PROGRAM
INTO ARCHITECTURAL
DESIGN, HIMMEL/
MKDG AND RTKL,
1984–86.

plans to a ULI "plan analysis session" in 1983, as a way of gaining an "over-the-shoulder" review of the program and plans by experienced developers and planners. Todd, with assistance from ULI staff, submitted a series of critical questions that focused on the vision of Reston Town Center as a new downtown. Todd asked, "Does any of the four alternative concepts offer the opportunity to create an economically viable retail/office center that can serve as the downtown at Reston?" The ULI panel's recommendations would fundamentally redirect the thinking of the town center. J. Hunter Richardson, marketing director at RLC, summarized the comments: "RLC has been too conservative and should be bolder. The driving force is the office component. Retail should follow. . . . The plans reflect a conflict. Is Town Center urban, or is it a high density suburban center? All agreed it should be more urban and the hotel [planned along the Dulles Toll Road] should be brought into the town center."[3]

In response, RTKL modified its plans during 1984–1986. It moved the hotel to the east end of town center and also anchored the west end of Market Street with a second hotel. In addition, the architects introduced a central focus—Fountain Square, an urban space framed by office buildings, retail stores, and a major hotel. Office and residential uses were integrated within the town center and structured parking complemented surface parking. Importantly, the basic skeleton of the future street pattern was evident. RTKL's 1986 plan featured a definite street grid and block pattern, a distinctly American urban form descended from colonial times.

Where the 1960s town center schemes separated cars and people with pedestrian underpasses, bridges, and greenways, the planners' aim in the mid-1980s was to organize buildings into the texture of a town composed of streets, public spaces, and the buildings defining them. At the same time, Robert Gladstone, now a Washington real estate developer who had advised Simon as an economic consultant in the 1960s, urged Reston Land to focus on the town center's urban design setting rather than the architectural design of individual buildings. In Gladstone's estimation, this was the way to create economic value and identity: "A strong, clear urban design framework for the entire Reston Town Center area needs to be conceived at the outset using key infrastructure elements to convey image and identity, at the same time allowing for wide architectural individuality at the scale of individual projects within the Town Center. A successful Town Center design on this basis can tolerate some mediocre individual buildings without damaging the total result." Gladstone had sought to partner with RLC to build Reston Town Center, and, while he did not succeed in this venture, he was responsible for a shift in thinking: An effective urban design plan could help create value. This grid of streets as the organizing principle marked a transition for Reston Town Center's planners.

DESIGNING AND BUILDING FOUNTAIN SQUARE, PHASE ONE: 1986–1990

By 1986 the new town of Reston was booming. The population had risen to 46,500 residents, and the apartment vacancy rate was a low 1.8 percent. Commercial space had increased over fifty percent in three years, to almost seven million square feet. As the Washington region expanded outward, Reston realized Robert Simon's original goal of a community with jobs as well as houses. This strong and growing critical mass gave Reston Land confidence to build the town center. With the RTKL plan in hand, RLC initiated the first phase.

For all its successes in building large-scale residential communities, RLC had limited experience developing at urban densities. The staging of construction, cash flow, and interdependent uses that the town center required was a world apart from low-rise land development. The ULI panel had recommended that RLC find a development partner well-versed with large urban projects and multiple uses. In 1984, after Jim Todd's departure and the promotion to president of Jim Cleveland, who had been on the Reston development team since Simon's days, Reston Land selected Ken Himmel/MKDG (Miller Klutznick Davis Gray) of Chicago to be its co-development partner. Himmel/MKDG's City Center project in Denver covered four blocks of high-rise offices and a luxury hotel on the city's street-oriented downtown. It was a model for the future Reston Town Center. Ken Himmel, developer of some of the generation's most successful mixed-use and retail projects, notably Boston's Copley Place and Chicago's Water Tower Place, would be instrumental in directing Reston's town center toward a downtown pattern with retail lining sidewalks and creating an animated urban street experience.

Jim Cleveland and Ken Himmel staged an architectural competition for the design of the twenty acres on which the first phase of the town center was to be built. The competition brief asked the architects to create a "memorable, vital, urban place" along the lines of the RTKL master plan. Entrants were well-established in the corporate and commercial market, including Kohn, Pederson Fox; Skidmore, Owings & Merrill; and Thompson Ventulett & Stainback. Mobil Reston, formerly Reston Land Corporation, also invited RTKL, which was already on board as Reston's master planner.

Skidmore Owings and Merrill (SOM), led by David Childs, presented a classically-inspired architectural ensemble centered around a perfect circular plaza, a space framing Reston Parkway to the east, and a crescent containing the composition to the west. Captivating eye-level renderings showed the public

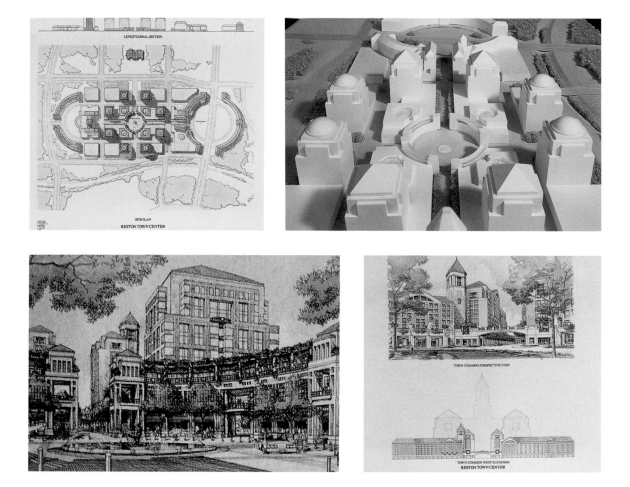

KEN HIMMEL DECIDED RTKL'S MASTER PLAN WAS LACKING IN ORIGINALITY AND SPIRIT, AND HOSTED AN ARCHITECTURAL COMPETITION BY "INVITATION ONLY." *ABOVE* SKIDMORE OWINGS & MERRILL PRESENTED A CLASSICALLY-INSPIRED ENSEMBLE CENTERED ON A CIRCULAR PLAZA.

KOHN PEDERSON FOX SUBMITTED A DESIGN THAT REFERRED TO THE CLASSICISM OF WASHINGTON IN A SCHEME ORGANIZED
AROUND AN ELONGATED CENTRAL PLAZA.

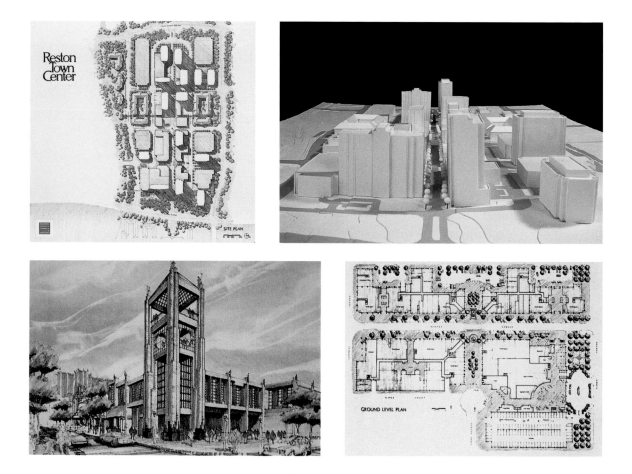

THOMPSON VENTULETT STAINBACK ILLLUSTRATED CONTEMPORARY BUILDINGS ALONG A MAIN STREET, A MORE RELAXED SCHEME COMPARED TO THE OTHER COMPETITORS.

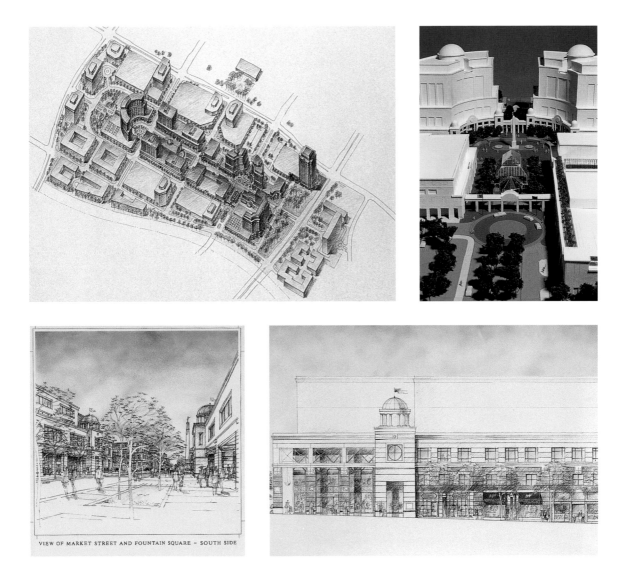

VIEW OF MARKET STREET AND FOUNTAIN SQUARE – SOUTH SIDE

RTKL ASSOCIATES FRAMED A CENTRAL PLAZA WITH BUILDINGS, ARCADES, AND PEDESTRIAN PASSAGES, WHILE EMPHASIZING AN OVERALL STREET AND BLOCK PATTERN.

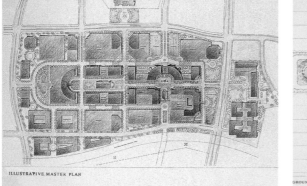

ILLUSTRATIVE MASTER PLAN

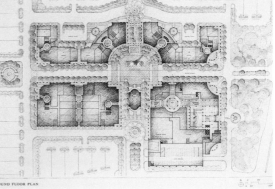

GROUND FLOOR PLAN

spaces framed by two- to three-story buildings with upper-level setbacks for vine-covered pergolas, shaded arcades, and pedestrian passages. Three-story towers extended over the sidewalks to help define the narrowed openings where the streets passed through the central plaza, containing the space with architecture. (A similar idea was expressed in the successful RTKL design.) However, the SOM design, while the most interesting architecturally, left little room to respond to programmatic differences in the shape and size of spaces and offered limited flexibility in the strict symmetry. Tom Grubisch, a Washington-area journalist who had written extensively on Reston, criticized the SOM design as a "too ambitious megadesign." In a 1987 *Architecture* magazine interview, Grubisch emphasized that the grandeur of SOM's proposal was inappropriate for the town center. "We have had enough of the almost totalitarian designs a la Le Corbusier. We need something more intimate than that."

Mobil Reston instead preferred RTKL's flexible and phaseable design and selected the architects to design the town center's first buildings. RTKL emphasized the street and block pattern, and amplified the planning and urban design principles they had established in earlier plans. While their scheme focused around Fountain Square, it was less rigid and not as strictly symmetrical as the SOM plan, providing adaptability for future development. This was appropriate for the sloping site with distinctly different streets planned around the edges of phase one. RTKL located a fountain on the north side of Market Street in the central square (later this would become the Mercury fountain), positioned to capture the longest sunlight exposure each day, and a small cultural building shown facing the fountain on the south side of Market Street. RTKL embraced an architectural attitude in this retrospective era, similar to the SOM design, that was influenced by the classicism of Washington, D.C.

LEFT RECONNAISSANCE PLAN OF TOWN CENTER LANDSCAPE, SHOWING THE EXISTING OAK TREE FOREST BEFORE CONSTRUCTION.

RIGHT SURVEYING THE TOWN CENTER LANDSCAPE SHOWED A RIDGE AND MATURE TREES ALONG RESTON PARKWAY, WHICH WAS ADAPTED TO A SITE FOR A PARK AND THE FOUNTAIN SQUARE BUILDINGS. *LEFT TO RIGHT*, CHUCK STEWART, VIRGINIA FOREST MANAGEMENT; GEORGE BURR, SASAKI; PAT LANIUS, RESTON LAND, OCTOBER 1987. SASAKI ASSOCIATES.

LANDSCAPE PLAN: 1988–1990

Sasaki Associates joined the design team in 1988 as landscape architects, working with RTKL on phase one of the town center. The design for the initial seven blocks was organized around a central plaza at Fountain Square, with Market Street as the town center's main street (although the street itself then ended in surface parking after two blocks, reserved for future development). As the real estate market improved in the mid-1980s, the phase one program was expanded to include 530,000 square feet of office space, 240,000 square feet of retail, and a 514-room hotel.[4]

As the designers focused on creating a dynamic commercial environment, Himmel and RLC developed a mixed-use program to bring life to the town center day and evening. Their plan aimed to energize the streets and side-

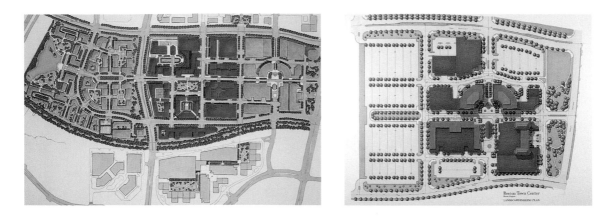

TOP LEFT SASAKI PLAN TO EXTEND RESTON TOWN CENTER URBAN CORE WESTWARD. A 5-MINUTE WALK WAS THE BASIC MEASURE OF PEDESTRIAN ACCESS WITHIN THE TOWN CENTER, NOVEMBER 1989. *TOP RIGHT* RESTON TOWN CENTER PHASE ONE SITE PLAN, WITH SURFACE PARKING ON FUTURE DEVELOPMENT SITES, RTKL AND SASAKI, DECEMBER 1989. *BOTTOM* SASAKI PERSPECTIVE OF URBAN CORE, NOVEMBER 1989. THE TOWN CENTER WAS ENVISIONED AS A SPECIAL URBAN PLACE, A "DOWNTOWN," SHOWN IN CONTRAST TO THE SURROUNDING URBAN GRID.

SASAKI'S PLAZA AND SIDEWALK STUDIES, JANUARY 1988. A PRELIMINARY DESIGN
FOR THE PLAZA SHOWED A FOUNTAIN FLANKED BY A PAIR OF SCULPTURAL PIECES.

walks with the mix of retail shops, restaurants, and multi-screen cinema. Ken Himmel reinforced this point in 2003: "When you talk about urban projects,... trying to create wonderful places, great places where people just want to spend time are driven to like a magnet, you're defining an environment and uses that have to include retail and restaurants."[5]

Market Street

Sasaki led the effort to determine the appropriate width and use of Market Street: the number of lanes; amount of on-street parking; sidewalk width; and planting space to create a good shopping street. It was to be the place for a mix of cars and people, not the main traffic route through the town center. Himmel provided input on street width to achieve comfortable sight-lines to retail stores on both sides—to enhance the visibility for pedestrians. Surface parking was designed for one side of the street only; parking on both sides would spread the buildings too far apart for the desired scale. With Himmel's concurrence, the designers visualized the street scene as being more about the storefronts (and pedestrians) than the ground-level architecture. RTKL and Sasaki created this variety by differing the storefronts, setbacks, awnings, and bay windows along the sidewalks.

Fountain Square

As the central focus of the new town center, Sasaki sought to refine the dimensions for this urban space. They prepared a series of scale comparisons to evaluate the size, an exercise designed to avoid making it too large. This was a major problem in designing a central urban plaza, as seen in the over-sized Boston City Hall Plaza, which rarely came to life. For Reston Town Center, Fountain Square was designed to feel comfortable when inhabited by only a few people or by a crowd-filled festival.

Market Street bisects Fountain Square to halve the size of the space and create intimate, human-scaled spaces on each side of the street. The slow-moving cars through the square also contribute to the activity of the town center. Sasaki's research confirmed that successful American urban spaces typically

ONE FOUNTAIN SQUARE, NORTH ENTRANCE. RTKL EMPHASIZED THE COMMERCIAL SCALE AND NATURE OF THE OFFICE BUILDINGS BY DESIGNING THE OFFICE ENTRANCES WITH A TWO-STORY, ARTICULATED FAÇADE AT THE BASE.

have cars at the edges and are framed by buildings. During outdoor events Market Street is closed and the Fountain Square opens to a single large plaza.

Two eleven-story office buildings define the north side of Fountain Square, their curving facades embracing the square. At the buildings' lower levels, arcades and two-story pavilions give further pedestrian scale and enclose Fountain Square. It is primarily a paved plaza, the brick extending across the street's surface. Retail shops and restaurants face the square to the south, with modest pedestrian-scaled entries to the office buildings. There is something symbolic in this urban fabric. Perhaps Fountain Square is too ordered, yet in the surrounding world of suburban disorder a bit more rigor may be necessary to define the larger Reston community's central place.

The stepped configuration of the Mercury fountain forms the central landmark feature of the square and the town center. A series of stepped water basins are built into the slope to help transition the grade up to a higher elevation on the north side of the square. An elevated circular basin of water forms the base for the iconic sculpture. Having reviewed the work of a dozen artists, Mobil Reston and Himmel/MKDG chose Brazilian-born sculptor Saint Clair Cemin to design a sculptural figure atop a spiraling, white marble column. The Mercury figure balances on one foot to bring a slight imbalance to the persistent symmetry of the buildings and fountain's base. After it was installed in summer 1993, *Washington Post* architecture critic Benjamin Forgey praised Mercury and its suburban setting: "On a typical summer evening," he wrote, "Reston Town Center is an upscale urban idyll: The rhythmic splashing of the Mercury fountain provides a background murmur as casually dressed people shop or window-shop along Market Street, or lounge at chairs and tables on warm red bricks of Fountain Square, or converse over wine and dinner outside." The journalist's comments provided insight into his own surprise by this distinctly urban place.

FOUNTAIN SQUARE
RESTON TOWN CENTER
SASAKI ASSOCIATES, INC.

WHITE-TABLECOTH
DINING UNDER THE
PLAZA TREES.

Green Spaces

The design of the urban spaces in phase one included the presence of nature as integral to the town center, one of the defining characteristics of American urbanism. Where European cities often have arcades to provide shelter in urban environments, the American counterpart has repetitive street trees for shade and to form a canopy. Sasaki planned shade trees along the street and within Fountain Square for environmental effects, as well as to define a pedestrian scale along the sidewalks and a zone for outdoor dining. The trees create a green roof over an outdoor plaza of movable chairs and tables during the day, transformed in the evening to a space for white-tablecloth dining.

Reston Park, fronting along Reston Parkway, is the soft green counterpoint to the paved plaza at Fountain Square. The town center's buildings are set back from the parkway, separating the urbanized area from the high-volume parkway by the park, a one-and-a-half-acre preserve of northern Virginia landscape. The park also creates the front door into the town center from the east and

THE CHERRY TREES IN BLOSSOM AT RESTON PARK.

establishes separation from high-speed traffic along Reston Parkway. Sasaki laid out paths and adjusted the grades at the edges of the park to meet the surrounding streets, and cleared understory vegetation to open up views from the parkway to the first buildings. Reston Park gave visibility through a landscaped setting to the street front shops at the end of Market Street. While the heart of the town center is focused inward along Market Street, the Hyatt Hotel with its porte-cochére opening out to Reston Park also extends the town center out to Reston Parkway.

Parking

Suburban development typically requires dedicated parking for each individual commercial building. The shared parking at Reston Town Center, by contrast, was planned along formulas for a typical downtown, with a shared inventory of spaces for all cars and a reduced number of required spaces overall. Even with the undeveloped parcels available for surface parking, Himmel urged Mobil Reston to build parking garages with the first buildings as a tangible gesture toward downtown densities.

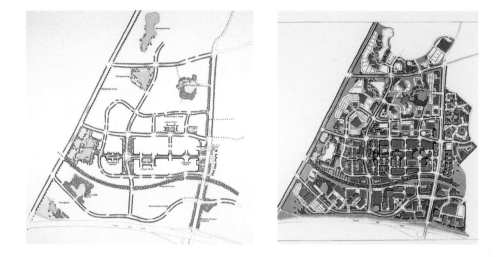

COMPLETING THE TOWN CENTER PLAN: 1990–2006

The first phase of Reston Town Center opened in 1990 to praise from the design and development community and an American Institute of Architects (AIA) urban design award to RTKL and Sasaki—the first of twenty-two planning and design awards at this writing. Sasaki transitioned to a broader role as town center planners and urban designers and began a series of planning and phasing studies to determine the logical sequence of building-out the balance of the town center core, or phase two, as it was called.

Mobil Reston's Thomas J. D'Alesandro IV, executive vice president, directed a strategy of building the next phases at the outer edges of the town center, preserving the key and most valuable closer-in parcels near Fountain Square. His aim was to capitalize on the value created by the existing development and to wait until the market matured to the urban densities called for in the key parcels planned for the tallest buildings. This strategy brought significant adjustments to the 1986 RTKL plan. Instead of Market Street extending on the west to a hotel, in this 1989–1991 plan Sasaki linked the heart of the town center around Fountain Square to a new high-density residential district. These would later become high-rise buildings. The expanded downtown fol-

LEFT

SASAKI PLANNING STUDY FOR THE LARGER 460-ACRE TOWN CENTER AREA SHOWING THE EXTENSION OF URBAN SPACES AND STREETS FROM THE CORE, AUGUST 1989.

RIGHT

ILLUSTRATIVE PLAN OF LARGER 460-ACRE TOWN CENTER AREA INCORPORATING EXISTING BUILDINGS TO THE NORTH AND SOUTH INTO THE TOWN CENTER PLAN, SEPTEMBER 1989.

lowing the street grid and sidewalks seemed a natural extension of the town center. (European commentators have remarked on the distinctly American idea of the grid extending out from the city to the horizon, not closed but open.) The revised Reston Town Center plan was the logical expression of a modern U. S. city.

Reston Town Square

D'Alesandro asked Sasaki to explore strategies to connect these outlying parcels to the Fountain Square area. Because the town center was surrounded by high-volume parkways, including six-lane Reston Parkway, the designers were constrained by existing conditions from extending the town center's urban design beyond the urban core, except west along the Market Street axis.

Sasaki developed urban design concepts for the extension of Market Street west, with a sequence of public spaces that built upon the ideas stated in phase one. As Market Street sloped westward along the parcels that would be developed after 1990, the town center evolved from the formality of the paved Fountain Square area to a slightly more relaxed urban plan with the green Reston Town Square on the south side of Market Street. Wisely RLC and Fairfax County agreed to remain flexible about the specific zoning and future land use around Reston Town Square, to enable the landowners to develop these blocks in response to prevailing market conditions at the time they were developed.

The centerpiece of Sasaki's plan was Reston Town Square, the one-acre park completed in 2005. It gave identity, both experientially and in real estate terms, to each of the blocks framing the square in this precinct of high-rise office and condominium buildings built between 1997 and 2006, including the 1,000 Midtown condominium units to the north and south. Sasaki completed a number of studies to determine the appropriate size for this green space, analyzing comparably-sized squares in urban neighborhoods, including Gramercy Park in New York, Lafayette Square in Washington, Rittenhouse Square in Philadelphia, and Johnson Square in Savannah, also about one acre,

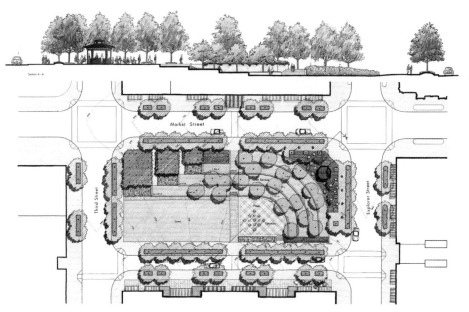

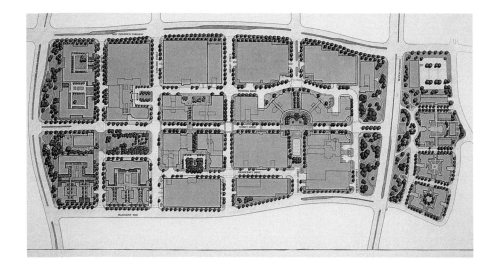

which proved to be the most appropriate for this context. Just as it was with Fountain Square, it was important to define the correct scale for the space to give a sense of vitality and activity, while also providing a usable refuge from the density of the surrounding blocks.

Freedom Square

For the next phase of Reston Town Center, architect William Hendrix of the Smith Group and Washington-based Sasaki considered the composition of buildings against the skyline, especially its visibility from the Dulles Toll Road. The first blocks west of the Fountain Square area, called Freedom Square, are at the geographic center of the urban core. To create a landmark in the skyline visible from the Toll Road, One Freedom Square, completed in 2000 at 18 stories and 400,000 square feet, was planned as the tallest building in Town Center. Two Freedom Square, completed in 2002, is 16 stories and also 400,000 square feet. These office towers were developed by Boston Properties and designed by the Smith Group.

An important difference between the unified architectural composition of the original Fountain Square development and the buildings clustered around Reston Town Square was the variety of design attitudes represented by multiple architects in the later works, similar to an evolving downtown. D'Alesandro posed these questions to the designers: How do you achieve continuity and draw aesthetic and pedestrian connections between these buildings?

D'Alesandro worked with Sasaki and the Smith Group to develop guidelines for treatments of the lower levels of buildings facing Market Street and extending around Reston Town Square. The alignment of a cornice, and a common palette and types of materials created visual continuity from one block to the next.

FREEDOM SQUARE
PLAZA.

A 24-Hour Neighborhood

Around Reston Town Square, Sasaki's 1990 plan called for mid-rise residential buildings bracketing the western end of Market Street, stepping down to low-rise townhouses across Town Center Parkway. In 2004 developer KSI Services, instead, envisioned the potential for more density, and set out to build 1,000 units in seven buildings, three of which are 21-story towers and two are 15 stories, built over streetfront shops and restaurants.

Town Center residents living within the urban core will number up to 2,500 people and create a 24-hour environment. Some critics have argued that Reston Town Center fails the test of an authentic downtown with its private streets that are governed and managed collectively by property owners. I would argue that a more accurate measure is the experience of the people who live, work, and shop at the town center.

Witold Rybczynski, writing in *Wharton Real Estate Review*, quantified the critical mass of people and density required to make a viable downtown. "The gross population density of that quintessential 24-hour place, Manhattan, is more than 80 persons per acre," he determined. "That is unusually high for an American city, but the density of compact San Francisco is 24 persons per acre, which probably represents a threshold for a viable 24-hour city."[6] Rybczynski defined a downtown area as the distance covered in a 20-minute walk from the city's center. Using this measure, by 2010 Reston Town Center within a ten-minute walk of Fountain Square will be home to 3,500 residential units and over 6,000 people (assuming 1.75 persons per unit). The town center area—covering the urban core and the blocks immediately across Reston Parkway, Fairfax County Parkway, and New Dominion Parkway—will have a gross population density of 75 persons per acre, or three times the density of San Francisco. This will no doubt look and feel like a downtown.

Rybczynski also addressed in the *Wharton* article the issue of critical, or total, population mass, requisite for a viable downtown. At Reston Town Center, is a population of 6,000 residents sufficient to support the basic retail infrastructure of a downtown—food markets, cleaners, other convenience and specialty

shops, as well as restaurants and take-out food shops? "There is no consensus about the exact number of people it takes to make a viable downtown," Rybczynski argued. "Ten thousand people is sometimes cited as the size of a neighborhood. But a successful downtown must be more than a neighborhood, it must support sufficient infrastructure to be a magnet for the surrounding city and region. My guess is that a downtown residential population closer to 40,000 persons is required to achieve a truly 'urban' scale."

Reston Town Center's residential base may not reach the critical mass of established downtowns, yet the densities of people on the streets, sidewalks, and public spaces that I have experienced, working as an urban designer and landscape architect in the town center, match the densities of older and vital downtowns. The overall Reston community is home to more than 20 million square feet of commercial space. This constitutes a significant employee base within a five-mile radius, a universe of approximately 80,000 people who use the town center during the workday, afternoons, and evenings. Urbanist Christopher Leinberger called it "a buzz" in his *Urban Land* article, "The Shape of Downtown," a situation in which there are enough people to create a dynamic, an appeal, where value creation is on an upward spiral. Someday, perhaps residents, daytime workers, and visitors will refer to it as "downtown."[7]

The inherent virtues of the messy vitality of older towns and cities that grew over time like natural phenomena, with a fabric of buildings connected with roads, cannot be underestimated. With the evolution of Reston Town Center, the question of whether it will approach the feel of a place that has had layers of development and change is unknown at this writing. Will it someday be a downtown that embodies the dreams and memories like other towns and cities in the past? Are irrational associations possible in a new downtown planned like Reston Town Center? Not yet, but in time, I hope so.

MARKET STREET BECOMES AN OPEN PEDESTRIAN PLAZA, CLOSED TO VEHICLES, DURING MAJOR FESTIVALS.

DEVELOPING
RESTON TOWN CENTER

THOMAS J. D'ALESANDRO IV

IT WOULD BE impossible to discuss Reston Town Center without first describing the extraordinary context out of which it came: the development of the new town of Reston. The launch of Reston in the early 1960s was unquestionably a heroic and optimistic initiative that made a massive and thus risky commitment to building an entire community according to aesthetic, social, and economic principles. Robert E. Simon expressed confidence that a private development team, newly formed, could build a new town that would have the creative and vibrant cultural life of a city while also preserving the natural serenity of the Virginia countryside. He assembled a team that understood they were embarking on a venture of far-reaching scope and expansive long-term goals. Reston would be an antidote to both urban decay and suburban sprawl. Being associated with a project of these dimensions shaped the development team's sense of possibility and responsibility. Simon set expectations high at the outset, and they remained high throughout Reston's development. The optimism that surrounded the creation of a new town was part of its history and identity.

THE VISION, ROBERT SIMON AND GULF OIL: 1964–1979

Simon anticipated a town center for Reston when planning began. While the original program was not built, it did establish that Reston would one day have a "downtown" and that Reston would not be a bedroom community. That there would be a town center also reflected the viewpoint of an actively engaged community of pioneer residents, people committed to Simon's vision who had opinions about what an ideal community's downtown should be.

The earliest residents began moving into Reston in 1964. Three years later, in 1967, Gulf Oil Corporation, then majority owner of Reston, would dismiss Robert Simon and express its intention to develop the community with a professional management team. Simon was a leader who articulated a distinct vision, but in Gulf's view he was not an astute manager capable of implementing the vision pragmatically. Thus the creator who had framed the Reston vision was no longer in control, and Gulf executives with no prior experience in nor passion for community development were taking over.

Pioneering residents were understandably alarmed. They worried that Gulf would abandon the vision and split the community into suburban subdivisions. In response, they formed the Reston Community Association (RCA) to monitor the developer's subsequent rezonings. (Reston was the first land development in the United States to implement community-wide zoning. To keep property taxes as low as possible for the owner, land remained under agricultural zoning until it was developed, then rezoned in alignment with the comprehensive plan adopted by Fairfax County.) The RCA, as well as the resident directors of The Reston Association, the homeowners association chartered to maintain Reston's natural open space and manage recreational programs, ensured that the citizens who had moved to Reston on the strength of its sophisticated vision and planned environment would have an effective voice in discussions about the community's future.

While predictable tensions existed between the developer and the citizens, they also shared an underlying affection for the community and a pride in shaping its history as they worked through the issues associated with building the community's defining institutions. Most of Gulf's development team, including Charles Veatch, William Lauer, and James Cleveland, lived in Reston and saw the place through residents' eyes. These individuals, too, adopted it as their home. It was more than merely a real estate investment. In spite of two changes in ownership control—from Simon to Gulf Oil, then Gulf Oil to Mobil Corporation—the development team remained in tact and continued to build the community in accordance with the comprehensive plan put in place by Simon, keeping the Reston vision alive.

CREATING A "SUNDAY AFTERNOON" PLACE, RESTON LAND CORPORATION: 1979–1987

When Mobil took over in 1979, the oil company changed the scope of the developer's operations. Simon and Gulf had built houses, retail centers, and office buildings themselves, in addition to developing the community infrastructure (streets, parks, utilities, residential lots, and pads for commercial development). Mobil, by contrast, limited its operations to land development, with the intention of selling it to others who would construct and manage buildings in Reston. It sold residential lots to homebuilders, land in the village centers to retail developers, and office sites to commercial developers.

Retail development within Reston's aesthetic guidelines proved a challenge. The commitment to conceal all uses behind forest-preserve screens greatly complicated the effort to bring in retailers that needed visibility. While the community program of clustering residential uses within natural settings was successful in attracting homeowners, the same principle worked against the viability of the neighborhood retail, or village centers.

Robert Simon had hoped to launch the town center early in Reston's development, and he understood that retail would play a pivotal role. He competed unsuccessfully, however, with Tysons Corner Center and its developer, Ted Lerner, for the critical anchor tenants required to launch the town center. This, in conjunction with the still small population of Reston, delayed the town center's development, eventually for more than 20 years. Even though they could have sold the land underlying the town center, Gulf and Mobil held the land until it could be developed in keeping with the comprehensive plan.

The opening of Dulles Toll Road in 1984 gave Reston a new advantage. The Dulles Airport Access Highway had run though Reston from the beginning, but it had no local access points. With the opening of the toll road, Reston's regional access improved dramatically and demand for office space in Reston exploded. Discussions about an office presence in the town center now became realistic. Meanwhile, the dramatic annual expansion of passenger traffic at Dulles Airport increased Reston's regional and national exposure. The

town center's proximity to the airport emerged as one of its main competitive advantages in the Washington metropolitan area office leasing market. Reston began its transition from bedroom community to regional employment center.

In the early 1980s Reston Land Corporation (RLC), the Mobil subsidiary developing Reston, began planning the town center in earnest. A team led by J. Hunter Richardson explored options, with the concept of an organizing spine, like an old-fashioned Main Street, gaining early support within RLC. The town center, as envisioned, would have a variety of uses, but primarily retail, organized along the main street. Working with Reston's lead architect and planner, William Elkjer, Richardson sought to create a "Sunday afternoon" place: with the rest of the week taken up by work and errands, they saw Sunday afternoon as Restonians' one unscheduled time. Town Center would have restaurants, retail, and offices to energize the area during the day, with the addition of cinema, a hotel and residences to energize the main street during the evening. People would join in the life of the community as it relaxed, populating Reston Town Center on Sunday afternoons, reading a book, drinking coffee, ice skating, pushing a baby stroller, or just people-watching.

In 1983, when Richardson and RLC took their initial thoughts to ULI, the ULI participants quite strongly endorsed the "main street" layout, but equally strongly believed that RLC's plan would not achieve its goal of creating a vibrant town center unless it radically increased the density of uses along the main street. Had RLC proceeded with the town center as initially conceived, it would have produced little more than what today is called a "lifestyle" center: ground-floor retail with two or three floors of office or residential space above.

Jim Cleveland, Elkjer, and Richardson asked RTKL to refine the plan. By 1985 the development program was sufficiently complex that RLC decided to joint venture in building Town Center—a departure from their usual practice of selling land for others to develop. It also was clear to RLC executives that they lacked the experience to develop hotel, office, and retail uses. They began interviewing potential development partners, but few developers could credibly argue that they had the capability to develop each use—residential, office, retail, civic, entertainment, hospitality, and so forth—in a manner that would come together as a unified place. Indeed, very few developers in the mid-1980s viewed Reston as an opportunity to create a new downtown for the existing community, let alone for northern Virginia, which was how Reston's developers envisioned the town center.

One developer emerged as accomplished in creating urbane places with a wide mix of uses, and that was Kenneth Himmel. He had led development of the Ritz Carlton at Water Tower Place in Chicago, then went on to lead development of all uses at Copley Place in Boston. He was looking for a suitable site in Washington, D.C., for high-quality hotel-retail-office-residential urban development. RLC and Himmel concluded that a partnership at Reston Town Center would afford each the opportunity to develop an integrated, urbane project that would be consistent with their desires and would stand out within the Washington market. Ken Himmel's expertise in urban place-making was what RLC sought in a partner, and Reston was an appropriate setting for Ken Himmel's ambitions.

Himmel was affiliated with the development firm MKDG, financed primarily by Marvin Davis. RLC formed a fifty-fifty partnership with Himmel/ MKDG to develop the first phase of Reston Town Center on 15 acres of the urban core. Himmel hoped that the partnership ultimately would extend over the entire 85-acre urban core, but RLC did not offer Himmel an option on the balance of the property.

As RTKL commenced design work on phase one, RLC continued its efforts to achieve zoning that would accommodate the town center as planned. Reston community leaders participated in the discussions, along with Fairfax County and Virginia state officials. There was a collective sense that the programmatic goals of the town center did not conform to any Fairfax County land-use zoning categories. With support from such citizen leaders as RCA chairman Janet Howell and Joseph Stowers, chairman of RCA's planning and zoning committee, and the leadership of a 20-year veteran of the Fairfax

County board of supervisors, Martha Pennino, and her planning commissioner, John Thillman, the county developed a new zoning category, "Planned Unit Development—Town Center," to accommodate town center development as it was designed. The zoning process represented a watershed accomplishment, enabling the town center's developers to build uses and densities as market conditions warranted. It also was a changing of the guard for RLC's law firm. It was the last major zoning action led by veteran attorney Edgar Pritchard, who had assisted Robert Simon in securing Reston's initial entitlements 25 years earlier, and the initial entitlement effort on the part of Mr. Pritchard's young associate Antonio Calabrese. Calabrese would manage all subsequent zoning actions at Reston Town Center.

Most of the discussion between the county and the developer focused on the county's desire for the developer to commit to substantial road construction within and surrounding the town center core. The zoning that Fairfax County approved in 1987 called for an elaborate network that addressed the Virginia Department of Transportation's goal of enhancing countywide north-south access. The result would be a widening of Reston Parkway that weakened the pedestrian connectivity between Town Center and Reston's villages. I regret that regional traffic demands had to be met in this way, particularly given the immediate proximity of Fairfax County Parkway on Town Center's western border. On the plus side, however, the comprehensive approach spelled out in the zoning application "proffers" enabled Reston Town Center to avoid the traffic congestion that would characterize such rival employment and shopping centers as Tysons Corner and Bailey's Crossroads. This would become a selling point for Reston.

MAKING MARKET STREET SPARKLE

The development team that Himmel/MKDG set up in Reston focused on the design, construction, and leasing of the first phase of Town Center, defined as four buildings along Market Street and around Fountain Square, three with office space above ground-floor retail and one hotel with ground-floor retail. Ken Himmel understood the tastes of affluent shoppers from his experiences on Chicago's Magnificent Mile and in Boston's Back Bay, and he developed a merchandizing plan responsive to the residents of northern Virginia. He augmented RTKL's Baltimore design studio, led by Frank Lucas, with other design expertise. Sasaki Associates, led by Alan Ward, designed the streetscape along Market Street and in Fountain Square. The office of Phil George developed storefront designs for the merchants along Market Street. RTKL's Washington studio, led by Rod Henderer, designed the hotel. This collection of architects gave the town center its civic beauty, the buildings framing an environment that completely distinguished Reston Town Center from its suburban peers.

Kenneth Wong of Himmel/MKDG led the day-to-day development process with an insistence on intense attention to detail. Street width, cornice lines, retail bay widths, and other dimensions of place were explored and debated thoroughly. Integrating multiple uses into single structures without unintentionally compromising any single use—an essential dimension of the design commission—required more thought than suburban commercial structures typically received. Anticipating how patrons would respond to Town Center, Ken Himmel communicated his vision of how each space would be experienced. "Ken and Ken" applied their hands-on knowledge of urban planning on a human scale and anticipated the growing affluence of Reston. We all understood that potential office tenants would want high-quality, varied experiences while hotel guests would have yet another set of standards for Reston Town Center to meet.

Today it might be tempting to view Reston Town Center within the context of the rhetoric of the Congress for the New Urbanism or as an early example of the "lifestyle centers" that have become ubiquitous. I would argue

that the special quality here grew out of the collaboration of the two partners, each of whom had expansive definitions of the development process and each of whom viewed the project as the complete "downtown" of a medium-sized city. Himmel brought an understanding of what was required to create a concentrated urban place, while Reston Land Corporation brought an understanding of how to plan the larger, 460-acre town center district in a manner that would integrate with and extend the character of that place. Reston Town Center reflected both what Himmel had learned at Water Tower and Copley Places and what the RLC team had learned at Reston's villages.

Leasing space was more of a challenge than designing it. When Reston Town Center took a booth at the 1989 International Council of Shopping Centers, James Rouse, among others, came by to look at the town center model. Mr. Rouse had developed dozens of shopping centers around the country, including some of the nation's first enclosed malls and such celebrated waterfront centers as Harbor Place in Baltimore and South Street Seaport in New York, yet he had not taken the step in his own new town, Columbia, Maryland, of making the town center more than a suburban mall surrounded by low-density uses. It was clear that Rouse didn't know what to think about the proposed program for Reston Town Center: his exclamation—"Good luck!"—certainly did not express a conviction that it would succeed.

Reston Town Center did enjoy one market advantage that a developer like Rouse could readily appreciate: Fairfax County had imposed the eight-mile zoning restrictions that limited the opportunity for a potential competitor to introduce regional retail nearby. The highly successful Tysons Corner Mall was eight miles to the east; Fair Oaks Mall was about the same distance to the south; to the west, the future Dulles Town Center Mall in Loudoun County also was about eight miles away; and to the north Reston was bordered by Great Falls's highly restrictive residential zoning. Inside this ring were some of the most affluent residents in the country, a condition that has only strengthened over time.

To merchandise retail leasing, the RLC–Himmel/MKDG partnership chose a strategy that balanced local and national merchants. The nationals have

TOP
MARKET STREET,
LOOKING WEST;
HYATT REGENCY
RESTON HOTEL *LEFT*;
FOUNTAIN SQUARE
AND FREEDOM
SQUARE OFFICE
BUILDINGS *RIGHT*.

BOTTOM
REGIONAL AND
NATIONAL RESTAU-
RANTS AND STORES
FILLED THE RETAIL
SPACE IN RESTON
TOWN CENTER'S
FIRST PHASE OF
DEVELOPMENT.

done very well since the early 1990s; Williams-Sonoma, Victoria's Secret, Pottery Barn, Origins, Banana Republic, Eddie Bauer, Talbot's and others have expanded into space vacated by local merchants who were unable to compete effectively.

OPENING THE TOWN CENTER: 1990

Despite the decline that beset Washington office and hotel markets since the start of construction in June 1988, the Fountain Square office buildings and the Hyatt Regency Reston opened in Fall 1990 to wide acclaim. Washington, D.C., had been considered "recession proof" prior to the late 1980s, due to steady annual increases in federal spending. So when governmental contracting leveled off in the late 1980s, it took developers time to recognize the shift; office buildings continued to be delivered in anticipation of new spending, job formation, and office demand. Office rents and hotel occupancies for every new development suffered.

Reston Town Center's office space did not lease up at the rental rates and pace originally forecast. The best performers at the launch of Town Center were the restaurants, the national retailers, and the cinema, which achieved sales volumes well in excess of original forecasts. But every use—office, hotel, retail, and restaurant—achieved sales and/or lease results that were 20 percent, on average, above their local peers.

Yet even with the advantages that Reston Town Center enjoyed, it was clear that 1990 rental rates for office space and regional hotel occupancies, as well as uncertainties about the financial health of local retail merchants in the town center, would postpone any plans for developing subsequent phases. The benefits of creating an alluring environment for office workers, shoppers, out-of-town visitors, and diners were clear, but the ongoing churning in the individual commercial markets meant that mixed-used development was a high-risk proposition. Reston Land Corporation received numerous inquiries about selling off remaining portions of the town center's core for single-use, lower-density projects, particularly from big-box retailers and multifamily homebuilders.

As the general manager of RLC, I regretted that the indefinite postponement of a second phase of Reston Town Center development meant the dismantling of Ken Himmel's team and the end of prospects for collaborating with them on subsequent buildings. In addition, Himmel's financial partner, Marvin Davis, decided to sell all Himmel/MKDG's commercial real estate holdings, including Reston Town Center. RLC bought out Himmel/MKDG in 1990, just prior to the opening of the Fountain Square buildings. Once again, Town Center's urban core was solely owned by Reston Land.

I hired some of the Himmel team to manage Town Center. Among those who agreed to stay was seasoned broker Joseph Ritchey. Ritchey had the distinction of having worked on the initial leasing of every new office building in Reston Town Center since 1986. He embraced the vision, and his personal enthusiasm paid off. Reston Town Center consistently enjoyed the highest rents and office occupancy rates in northern Virginia.

Also hired from the Himmel team was Randa Mendenhall, who had responsibility for events in Reston Town Center. Through her efforts and the efforts of Linda Miller, Reston Land's marketing director, the town center hosted signature events consistent with its status as the social center of Reston. Events inaugurated on their watch included the Northern Virginia Fine Arts Festival, now rated nationally among the best outdoor art fests; the holiday parade; the Fountain Square summer concert series; Octoberfest, and Best of Reston, an event sponsored by the Greater Reston Chamber of Commerce that raises hundreds of thousands of dollars for social programs.

One aspect of Reston Town Center's first phase illustrates the limits of planning and the merits of maintaining flexibility to respond to evolving situations. Town Center zoning called for development of a "cultural center" on the southern half of Fountain Square. I took on responsibility for resolving the program for the building, which was envisioned as a gallery, and commissioned the Atlanta-based architectural firm Scogin Elam & Bray. Principal architect Mack Scogin believed that the open space of Fountain Square should not be "filled" by a museum building, and his proposed design raised the galleries on "stilts," leaving ground level as open as possible.

The presentation of Scogin's cultural center designs to Wolf Tiersch, the senior architect at Reston Land's parent, Mobil Corporation, was the most explosive meeting I have witnessed in my entire career. Tiersch's violent reaction to the design stunned everyone, and, happy still to be employed at the conclusion of the conference, I quickly moved on to plan B. I commissioned a second design for the gallery from the New York firm Hardy Holzman Pfeiffer. They designed an elegant gallery building that anchored the space, as most people would expect of a museum.

While the programming and design efforts progressed, Hunter Richardson advanced the notion of putting in a temporary ice rink to hold the space in winter. The rink was immensely popular and demonstrated the soundness of Mack Scogin's instinct—Fountain Square worked well as an expansive open plaza. The ice rink experience, in conjunction with the popularity of the

first season of summer concerts, led us to relocate the gallery and instead erect a structure that would serve as an ice rink in winter and a bandstand in summer. RTKL was brought back to design the pavilion that both anchors the square and preserves its openness. This third design was greeted with enthusiasm by the owners, who were exhausted by the cultural center discussion.

OUTSIDE THE CORE

I reserved the balance of the urban core of Town Center until that time when demand would support the development of multiple uses at the original town center densities. This was an effort to bring residences into the larger town center district, bounded by Reston Parkway, Baron Cameron Avenue, Fairfax County Parkway, and Dulles Toll Road. It was clear to all participants in the planning that the vitality we sought would be enhanced when people not only worked and shopped but also lived there.

Reston Land also wanted to merchandize retail beyond what we could place on Market Street in order to attract grocery and other larger-footprint merchants, such as Barnes & Noble and Best Buy. The fashion merchants on Market Street were not all doing as well as we had hoped, and we concluded that Market Street alone could not achieve the critical mass and

THE SPECTRUM RETAIL DISTRICT *RIGHT* AND PARAMOUNT CONDOMINIUM *LEFT* ARE NORTH OF RESTON TOWN CENTER'S URBAN CORE AND REINFORCE THE CRITICAL MASS OF SHOPS AND HOUSING, RESTON PARKWAY, *RIGHT*.

WEST MARKET
TOWNHOUSES.

mix of shops needed to establish Reston Town Center as the retail destination our goals required.

To address these two concerns, I launched a number of initiatives. I
worked with Al Hagelis, who had taken Elkjer's former role as Reston senior
planner after Elkjer moved into Wolf Tiersch's position at Mobil when Wolf
retired, to redraw Market Street to extend a few blocks westward (past Town
Center Parkway through to the 50-acre parcel of land known as West Market).
This revision would permit construction of more than 2,000 residential units
along Market Street in the western portion of the urban core and in the neighborhood of West Market.

During the early 1990s new development in Reston Town Center continued on land parcels surrounding the urban core. The first Town Center residential project, the 180-unit Oak Park Condominium on the north side of New
Dominion Parkway, sold out within a year at a record pace among its competitors, proving the attractiveness of living proximate to Market Street. Oak
Park's developer, the Peterson Companies, went on to develop Edgewater just

northwest of Oak Park, thereby expanding the residential program by another 250 units. Leading Oak Park's development was a former RLC president, James Todd. Todd had left Reston shortly after giving Hunter Richardson the charter to plan Reston Town Center. His confidence in the plan motivated him to bring in his new firm to launch the residential program.

To address the need for more-expansive retail offerings, Reston Land sold several acres just north of the urban core to Lerner Enterprises, which developed 250,000 square feet of retail and restaurants named The Spectrum. Peter Henry, the leader of Lerner's efforts, brought the upscale grocery store Sutton Place Gourmet (now Balducci's) into Town Center, as well as merchants offering men's and women's clothing, books, and electronics. His efforts more than doubled the amount of shopping and dining in Town Center and helped to achieve the "critical mass and mix" needed to sustain a regional retail destination. Development of The Spectrum had met with opposition from Reston founder Robert Simon, who believed that after The Spectrum all future development throughout the 460-acre Reston Town Center district should have a high density of mixed uses.

In the mid 1990s planning began for the West Market residential neighborhood bordering Town Center Parkway. The parcel initially had been viewed as suitable for industrial uses, but the plans prepared by Sasaki Associates for a residential neighborhood attracted strong interest among homebuilders. Reston Land held a competition among homebuilders for lots at West Market, and Chicago architect George Papageorge's townhouse design for Miller & Smith so impressed us that we awarded to Miller & Smith twice as much land as we had intended to allocate to townhouses. The finished units, reminiscent of new construction in Chicago's in-town neighborhoods, would be West Market's strongest sellers and further elevated the urbanity of Reston Town Center.

PLANS FOR EXPANDING THE URBAN CORE
AND FUTURE DEVELOPMENT

RLC interviewed architects for subsequent phases, reflecting the owner's belief that Reston Town Center would be enhanced by commissioning designers who could approach the project from a fresh perspective, not for dissatisfaction with RTKL. Sasaki was retained to provide continuity between design phases. In 1992, we commissioned Washington-based Keyes Condon Florance (KCF) to design the next phase of Town Center, the Freedom Square buildings. When office leasing picked up again, these plans would give Reston Land a competitive advantage: we would be able to present prospective tenants with a lease proposal for a building that was already designed. Architect Colden (Coke) Florance understood that the second phase of Reston Town Center would be the center of the urban core, and he responded by proposing what was expected to be Town Center's tallest building. Though only a fraction of the height of the romantic, soaring towers in America's biggest cities, 18-story One Freedom Square effectively referenced the Art Deco style of the most popular skyscrapers of the early 20th century, and it confirmed our view that Reston Town Center could credibly express an urban chic.

When Simon began Reston, he envisioned a series of "skyscrapers," and Heron House, the 14-story residential tower that he developed in 1964, expressed his intention for Reston to have buildings of monumental and heroic height to distinguish it as a new town, not a suburban community.

In the early 1990s RLC also asked Sasaki to design Reston Town Square, the second major park in the urban core. Land had been set aside in order to have multiple open spaces that serve as focal points in Town Center. One model was Savannah, Georgia, and Oglethorpe's plan for a series of town squares, each with a particular character, that define neighborhoods and make the city one of the most pleasant for walking. The town center's network of public places—Reston Town Square joining Fountain Square, Freedom Square, Library Park, Market Street, and the adjacent Discovery

THE 18-STORY ONE
FREEDOM SQUARE
TOWER, HEADQUAR-
TERS OF ACCENTURE.

Square on the south—established its civic balance of public and private spaces. The conceptual design for this next phase of development was completed in 1993, and Joe Ritchey used it to promote office leasing in the four proposed buildings.

BUILDING PHASE TWO: 1996–2003

In 1996 Mobil Corporation sold its interest in Reston, one among the 22 master-planned communities that it had been developing, to Westbrook Partners. They named the new company Terrabrook. (Westbrook had not acquired the four buildings of Reston Town Center phase one: Blackstone, an investment group, acquired the Hyatt Regency Reston; Equity Office Properties, a real estate investment trust, acquired the Fountain Square office buildings.) The urban core once again had disparate ownership. Most Reston Land Company employees joined Terrabrook to continue the development of Reston and its town center.

There was a consensus that all future buildings in the urban core should have mixed uses. We believed, however, that single-use buildings outside this area in the larger town center district would enhance the vitality of the urban core. Our goal was to increase the number of workers and residents within walking distance and thereby strengthen its ability to function viably. The success of the first neighboring residential developments encouraged us.

Terrabrook saw the advantage of developing property in Town Center rather than selling it to others, just as Mobil saw the advantage of partnering with strong developers who could augment the skills of the local team. With this in mind, Terrabrook formed a partnership with Boston Properties to co-develop a series of office buildings, including One and Two Freedom Square in the urban core; and, on Town Center land to the west and outside the core, One and Two Discovery Square and One and Two Reston Overlook. Boston Properties' excellent reputation in Washington as an office developer and landlord was in large part due to the efforts of executive vice president Raymond A. (Ray) Ritchey. Ritchey had confidence, based on the success of the first office

DISCOVERY SQUARE
AND RESTON
OVERLOOK, VIEWED
FROM THE TOWN
CENTER'S PEDES-
TRIAN BRIDGE.

LEFT
ONE FREEDOM
SQUARE, *RIGHT*, AND
TWO FREEDOM
SQUARE, *LEFT*, ALONG
MARKET STREET.

RIGHT
FREEDOM SQUARE
STREETFRONT
RESTAURANTS AND
SHOPS.

buildings, that Reston Town Center could emerge as the highest-quality corporate address in northern Virginia. He saw an opportunity to build a more attractive alternative to Tysons Corner, where a number of established developers, including Lerner Enterprises and West Group, owned the best remaining undeveloped land. Boston Properties could best compete by establishing a large presence in another Virginia market, and Reston fit the bill.

The partnership with Boston Properties was expected to be favorable due in part to BP's contacts with downtown office tenants. Indeed, these contacts became immediately significant when in 1997, after a four-year lull in the office market, a large Washington-based tenant, Andersen Consulting (incorporated as Accenture) requested proposals from Virginia developers to build them a new headquarters. The plans for the Freedom Square office tower were opportune. Based on the design for One Freedom Square by KCF, now The Smith Group, Andersen Consulting selected Terrabrook/Boston Properties to build them a new regional headquarters. With their lease commitment, Reston Town Center's future development commenced. Our primary competitors, Tyson's Corner developers, had been confident that their location eight miles closer to the District of Columbia would ensure their success, yet the urbanity of the town center outweighed the value of proximity to downtown Washington.

The selection of Town Center by a tenant of Accenture's stature led industry leaders to reassess its significance as an employment center for higher-profile firms. For the first time, Reston Town Center began to secure leases with national law firms with technology practices, as technology employment grew in northern Virginia, including Cooley Godward, Wilson Sinsini, and Latham Watkins. Reston Town Center met the law firms' requirements for an urbane setting.

In order to ensure that the second phase of Reston Town Center would have the same level of quality for all of its uses, Terrabrook hired Richard Heapes of Streetworks to supervise design of One Freedom Square's ground-floor retail space. He also designed the streetfront retail in Two Freedom Square.

Joe Ritchey of Terrabrook quickly leased One Freedom Square's remaining space. (Accenture planned to occupy about half the building.) Terrabrook and Boston Properties began designing Two Freedom Square as a 16-story office building with ground-floor retail and restaurants. The defense contractor Titan leased most of that space, and the law firm Finnegan Henderson Farabow Garrett and Dunner took the balance. By 2000 six new office buildings were under development in the larger Town Center area—the two Freedom Square towers on Market Street, two buildings along Dulles Toll Road on the east side of Reston Parkway for the software giant Oracle, and two buildings at Reston Overlook on the west side of Reston Parkway, across from Oracle, for the government contractor BDM.

Without question, Reston Town Center had captured the attention of firms considering a location in the Dulles corridor, from Tysons Corner to beyond Dulles International Airport, and was beginning to be seen as its urban core. The Dulles corridor had become "Main Street" for high-technology firms in Virginia, housing major offices of AOL, MCI, Nextel, Sprint, and other internet and telecommunications companies, along with their law firms and consultants.

THE EMERGING RESIDENTIAL NEIGHBORHOOD

Reston Town Center was also emerging as a residential neighborhood. For some time in the early 1990s, Albert Small, Sr., founder of Southern Engineering that developed the highly acclaimed Somerset House condominium towers in Chevy Chase, Maryland, and one of Washington's most distinguished residential developers, had been in discussions with Reston Land about developing a high-rise residential tower on nine acres on the east side of Reston Parkway. The site's location at the eastern end of the Market Street view corridor gave it a special prominence; any structure there would have a strong visual presence in the urban core.

Small's timing was fortuitous: An agreement between Reston Land and another homebuilder failed to reach settlement. To secure a commitment from a developer to build a high-rise there, Reston Land was willing to make some compromises. RLC/Terrabrook agreed to allow Small to build mid-rise residences on the balance of the site. The agreement also called for Terrabrook to receive a portion of revenues from the developer's condominium sales. Albert Small's Stratford House on Reston Parkway overlooked the town center's Market Street, and units in the high-rise building outsold the adjacent mid-rise condos. Designed by Chevy Chase architect John Torti, Stratford House established Reston Town Center's attractiveness to people looking for an urban place in the suburbs.

Given Stratford House's success, we began looking for a partner for residential development inside the urban core. We decided to target rental apartments on the western-most block, because of the established condominium presence at West Market and Stratford House. Rental units, we believed, would attract young professionals, empty nesters, and other people with a different profile from condominium buyers, which in turn would help create a vital mix of residents attractive to employers in the office buildings and to merchants on Market Street.

We invited proposals from seven apartment developers. Three proposed mid-rise buildings with structured parking; three others proposed high-rise development with structured parking; and one, Trammell Crow Residential (TCR), proposed a mid-rise complex with underground parking, which Terrabrook selected. Despite higher costs for underground garages, the arrangement would allow 700 units on the seven-acre site, almost double what would have been possible with above-grade parking structures. Mid-rise buildings would be less expensive to build than high-rise structures, and we believed that premium rents could be achieved in Reston Town Center without additional heights. (As we have seen, the residential market has continued to evolve, and the recently completed Midtown towers have underground parking and high-rise construction, reflecting a cost structure that made Terrabrook apprehensive even around 2000.)

Terrabrook and TCR, a national developer who had experience with projects of this nature, established a partnership to develop 700 apartments. We began design with Chris Lessard of Virginia-based Lessard Group Architects. As development progressed, two changes led to the units being developed partially as condominiums and solely by TCR. First, as the start of construction approached, land values appreciated to the extent that Terrabrook decided to sell to TCR rather than participate in development. Second, declining interest rates had enhanced the market for condominiums.

FILLING IN THE CENTER

Trammell Crow's construction of residential units on the western portion of the urban core was consistent with Terrabrook's desire to complete the town center by developing the central portion last. The parcels at the geographic center had been held back until the market could support higher densities and,

OPPOSITE
THE ICE SKATING
RINK IN THE RESTON
TOWN CENTER
PAVILION BECOMES
A DESTINATION
DURING THE
HOLIDAYS.

thus, higher value. These blocks would support a special program if we first allowed Town Center to develop around it. Our original intention to develop a second full-service hotel, in addition to the Hyatt, had given way to economic realities: the hospitality industry, very hard hit by the dot.com bust of Spring 2000, had been further devastated by the terrorist attacks of 9/11 in 2001. Fortunately, zoning in Reston Town Center was flexible enough to allow Terrabrook to respond to market opportunities. Interest in living in the emerging urban neighborhood had continued to expand.

Terrabrook, technically an investment fund of Westbrook Partners, faced time pressures to divest of its holdings. By 2002, it became clear that it would be impossible for Terrabrook to develop additional buildings given the divesture timetable. We thus moved to sell off the remaining town center parcels, in lieu of participating in development.

Terrabrook's executive responsible for commercial land sales, Gary Modjeska, began a competitive process to sell the remaining parcels, for residential, retail, and hospitality uses. Four bidders submitted proposals. KSI, a prominent local developer of both high-density and large-scale communities, hired Lessard to prepare its program. Together, Robert C. Kettler and Chris Lessard successfully anticipated the option that Terrabrook found most satisfying: a residential neighborhood with style and density. Midtown is a romantic response to urban living, and the two twenty-one-story towers elegantly complete the urban core's residential program while reaching the highest densities in all of Reston. Terrabrook selected KSI on the strength of its program, and a contract for the sale of 6.13 acres finalized in 2003.

As the year began, Westbrook Partners accelerated their exit from Reston Town Center. In the spring they sold their interest in One and Two Discovery Square to Boston Properties, then that summer sold BP their interest in One and Two Freedom Square, along with the last remaining undeveloped block in the urban core. The last pieces of the Reston development puzzle fell into place when Equity Office Properties began a process of redeveloping the first phase of Reston Town Center property.

The commitment and decisions of Reston Land and Terrabrook to create a high-quality urban environment at the center of Reston have paid dividends not only in financial returns to the developers, but in the quality of life of the people who live, work, shop, and dine there.

ENDNOTE

On a personal note, Terrabrook's shift in 2002 from developing Reston Town Center to selling their land holdings made it clear that my career with Reston Town Center, begun 20 years earlier, was coming to a close. When the opportunity to lead development of The Woodlands in Texas presented itself, I knew it was time to move. The Woodlands is a master-planned community designed on the Reston model. The town center was still substantially undeveloped and had the potential of being even more vibrant than Reston's. I looked forward to taking what I had learned from the exemplary developers, builders and architects who had contributed to Reston Town Center and applying it to a new venue, one with a rich history of its own. I also looked forward to learning still more from working with the accomplished team at The Woodlands.

It has been a privilege to be a part of Reston Town Center's initial development. Perhaps one day I will return there to live. I would continue to watch Town Center with interest, certain that Reston will continue to provide new models for American urbanity.

Rachel S. Cox, a freelance writer based in Washington, D.C., contributed to this chapter.

BUILDING AN
URBAN NEIGHBORHOOD

ROBERT C. KETTLER

THE FIRST TIME I walked the Reston Town Center construction site in the late 1980s I was struck by the revolution taking place. In comparison to the strip commercial development lining the byways of America, this town center's mixed-use design exhibited what became the cutting edge of suburban development and redevelopment. Nothing in the area hinted of a city center, but that is exactly what Reston Town Center aimed to be—an urban core in an un-urban location. When it opened in 1990, the fusion of street retail, hotel, restaurants, offices, entertainment, and public gathering spaces, was just as attractive on a smaller scale as downtown Washington's best urban neighborhoods. There was a magical human scale and genuine finish to the buildings that kept a close relationship to the street for drawing in customers. Although this urban island seemed strangely out of place in a suburban sea, the potential of the project hit me. People could work, sleep, eat, and play in one place without buckling their seatbelts. And they could do it in the suburbs.

Industry observers at the time acclaimed the project as visionary yet criticized it as an economic folly by developer Mobil Oil. They believed the market would not pay the premium for the town center's structured parking and public improvements, compared to the suburban competition offering surface parking, few amenities, and lower rent. Market critics completely discounted the convenience, and quality-of-life benefits that existed in this (and other) energizing mixed-use environments.

As everyone recognizes today, the project became an incredible success for owners, tenants, and people. The office buildings around Fountain Square commanded premium rent and achieved the lowest vacancy rate of any competing property, in spite of the withering office recession of the early 1990s.

The Hyatt Hotel also recorded the highest market occupancies at the time, thanks to business from the town center and nearby offices and the attraction of the constant street activity outside its doors.

The retail shops also claimed the most success of any comparable retail development in the Washington market, then and now commanding the highest rents and sales per foot. Opening rents averaged 25 to 30 percent higher than market and have maintained that margin above the competition. Most of the space had been leased prior to opening, and rarely have stores been vacant in the past ten years. The addition of Freedom Square in 2002 doubled the amount of first-class office space and added significantly to the retail and restaurant mix.

The town center is safe, clean, dynamic, and people love it. Sidewalk cafes, restaurants, entertainment, and shops spill together in welcoming plaza spaces where daytime workers take a break for lunch or coffee in the region's only authentic, mixed-use urban environment. People-watching and meeting friends and neighbors on the street are commonplace. Reston Town Center completely departs from the standard system of Euclidean zoning in which housing, office, retail, and entertainment are quarantined in separate precincts. By 2003, Reston Town Center had become a multi-owner day and night place and now included medium-density condos and early versions of urban-style townhouses. In short, the town center had developed the critical mass necessary to make high-density condominium development feasible.

LEFT
MARKET STREET SIDEWALKS, PLANTING, AND ONSTREET PARKING.

RIGHT
PINK PALM SHOP IS ONE OF RESTON TOWN CENTER'S MANY BOUTIQUES.

AN URBAN MARKET IN THE SUBURBS

After winning a design competition, KSI contracted to purchase 6.13 acres in Reston Town Center in 2003 with the vision of building 1,000 high-rise residential units. At that time, we were alone in believing that high-end, high-rise condominiums and apartments could be successful and feasible. Our research and experience showed indications of a growing market of buyers and renters with urban tastes.

We have come to learn that changing housing tastes—due to aging baby boomers; the cultural impact of immigrants familiar with urban life; the higher percentage of single households; couples having children at later ages; and the desire for a shorter commute—are feeding demand for pedestrian-oriented urban communities. Reston Town Center is unique simply because of where it is: the suburbs. What it proves is that it can happen anywhere jobs, transportation, shopping, and place-making urban design occur. This is good news for the future of America's suburbs.

It was the experience early in my career renovating places in and around the neighborhoods of Georgetown and Adams Morgan that solidified my belief in the power of pedestrian-oriented communities. The people who bought in these city places tended to be young, educated, artsy, single professionals who wanted a sophisticated lifestyle in an affordable, urban environs. They desired exposed brick, high ceilings, restored trim, open floor plans, mass transit, and the ability to walk to work, to restaurants, the grocery store, and to go out with friends. They really lived and worked in their neighborhoods and shared in the culture and nightlife by strolling down the street or heading to the nearby Metro station.

In the nearly three decades since then, a much larger and growing urban-oriented market has evolved throughout the Washington region, due to a unique variety of factors. One variable is a growing labor force that brings in thousands of smart, educated people each year. In 2004 alone, the Washington metropolitan area added 78,000 jobs to the market—second in the nation for job growth, just behind the New York region. Many of these jobs were in the

DAYTIME WORKERS
AT THE FREEDOM
SQUARE AND
FOUNTAIN SQUARE
OFFICE BUILDINGS,
PLUS NEARBY
DISCOVERY SQUARE
AND RESTON
OVERLOOK,
PATRONIZE
TOWN CENTER
RESTAURANTS AND
SHOPS THROUGHOUT
THE WEEK.

services and government sectors. Also, government and government contractors provided a giant research and development engine for the Washington economy, having the same impact on the Washington-area employment market as Stanford University and UC/Berkeley have on northern California and MIT and Harvard have on the Boston area.

Major companies like Capital One, AOL, Exxon–Mobil, and American Management Systems are located within five miles of Reston. Northrup Grumman, Titan, Oracle, Accenture, and Sallie Mae have headquarters offices within Town Center itself. These companies and others employ affluent, multicultural, urban-oriented homebuyers and renters who want to live near their jobs to avoid road congestion and lengthy commutes.

Furthermore, over 91,000 new people are slated to live in Fairfax County by 2010. With no low-density suburban land left, where will they live? They require a new type of living environment, and Reston Town Center is a part of the answer.

Other factors that influence the changing demand and taste in housing are income and heritage. More Washington-area residents have advanced degrees than any other metropolis in the country. Eight of the nation's 30 wealthiest counties—more than 25 percent—are located in this region. In Fairfax County alone, over one-third of households are in the top income brackets. As with other booming "melting pot" cities like New York, Los Angeles, and Miami, the Washington area is one of diversity. Seventeen percent of residents were born in foreign countries and bring to their Washington lives ethnic tastes, trends, and cultures. Twenty percent do not speak—or think—in English. According to Harvard's Joint Center for Housing Studies in its State of the Nation's Housing 2004 report, "one in ten [area] households is now headed by a person born outside the United States."[1]

Another factor is cultural and professional aptitude. The "creative class" is what George Mason University's Richard Florida calls the rising number of people dominating Washington's growth. He defines them as people in "science and engineering, architecture and design, education, arts, music and entertainment whose economic function is to create new ideas, new technology, and new creative content." They want 24-hour access to the global market and to mass transit—to be where they want, when they want, any time of day or night. Florida ranked Washington the number-one destination for the creative class, with 40 percent of all jobs there in this realm. And indeed, they thrive in a setting just like Washington: densely populated, a growing job-base, quality products, diversity, and culture.

A SEVERELY LIMITED SUBURBAN HOUSING SUPPLY

This complex dynamic of factors is occurring in an increasingly congested metropolis of 5.9 million people living on scarce, expensive, and highly-regulated land. The Chesapeake Bay on the east and south are insurmountable physical boundaries, with environmental and political boundaries on all edges. For example, the buildings in which many Washingtonians now live and work would not be allowed to be built under current wetlands regulations. The counties surrounding Washington, D.C.—Montgomery, Loudoun, Prince Georges, and Prince William—have down-zoned and restricted land-use along their edges, in vast and virtually unbuildable 5-to-20-mile-wide buffers. This has created a huge, low-density belt around the city and further limited housing options.

In addition, the region's builders and developers are unable to keep pace with the rate of job growth due to the time it takes to process entitlements and permits. Due to these largely political constraints, the region's real estate industry can engineer and entitle 37,000 housing permits annually, far less than job growth warrants. George Mason University economists predict that the demand for housing units in the Washington area is expected to outstrip supply by up to 20,000 units per year through the end of the decade.

Across metropolitan Washington, raw land values have soared up to 1,000 percent over the five-year period, 2000–2005. Some suburban areas, in fact, have evolved rapidly from affordable, starter-home locations to luxury venues, particularly if they have detached houses accessible to transit and are

within a community offering a full complement of amenities, services and evolving employment opportunities.

However, despite scarcity and high prices, the Washington region for now remains quite affordable relative to northern California, and the New York City and Boston regions—all highly attractive employment markets. In contrast to housing in these other areas, metropolitan Washington is more affordable. In 2003, it ranked 26th nationwide in the number of million-dollar homes. California was number one, with New York right behind.[2] In fact, the ratio of housing costs to incomes could just about double for the Washington area before its reaches California and New York levels.

GOING VERTICAL

The response to all of these factors is to build vertically.

Today's suburbs are undergoing redevelopment that generally aligns with downtown living environments. Reston Town Center's owners planned this from the beginning. In increasing numbers, suburban developers (and public planning offices) are abandoning Euclidean models of development, which required huge road-building projects and created sprawl, and in their place favoring high-density, mixed-use, transit-oriented programs. They are making a dramatic shift to a vertical product as the realities of a finite land supply collide with constant and overwhelming demand.

In spring 2003, Terrabrook approached KSI about buying 6.13 acres in the urban core for residential development. Terrabrook's Tom D'Alesandro had seen our work in Pentagon Row just a mile across the Potomac from Washington, D.C., and adjacent to the Pentagon complex. Pentagon Row and Pentagon East, adjacent mixed-use projects of shopping, eateries, and living spaces are being built at a residential density of 4,000 units on 20 acres—200 units an acre. Terrabrook viewed KSI's dense-development experience and zoning expertise as ideal for Reston Town Center.[3]

Of the 30 companies asked to bid on the land at the town center, only KSI proposed high-rise residential structures. We won the project development rights for the urban design of the Midtown neighborhood, what we called a "vertical planned community." It packaged the elements of a traditional, low-density community in a vertical context of seven high-rise buildings: two, 21-story towers with 293 condos and 16,000 square feet of restaurants, health club, and shops; an adjacent 21-story apartment building with 288 units; 78 high-ceilinged lofts in a seven-story building; and 341 condos and 34,000 square feet of shopping space in the last building rising 15 stories. The Midtown neighborhood is anchored by a 1.25-acre urban park, a green counterpoint to Fountain Square's hard-scape, a natural gathering place, and a community amenity for homeowners overlooking the green or the public watching a live-art performance.

OPPOSITE
THE 21-STORY
MIDTOWN EAST
AND WEST TOWERS
LEFT RISE ABOVE
FREEDOM SQUARE
ONE *RIGHT* AND TWO
CENTER.

The Midtown neighborhood was conceived to respond to a rising demand for multifamily living in Washington's suburbs, as well as nationwide, based on the 2000 U.S. Census. In less than a decade, multifamily housing permits in Fairfax County (where Reston Town Center is located) and Maryland's Montgomery County (which includes Bethesda and Silver Spring) have doubled from 20 percent of total home construction in the 1990s to over 40 percent in 2005.

This signals a change in taste and available product. By and large, 20- and 30-somethings and baby boomers, empty nesters, and retirees do not want to mow the lawn or shovel snow. Cashing in on the housing boom fueled by low interest rates, several apartment building owners have also begun converting rental units to condominiums. Trammel Crow Residential even shifted mid-construction to accommodate the market and build-out The Savoy units for sale rather than for rent.[4]

The urban-style loft is a variation of this. With open floor plans, high ceilings, and spacious windows, lofts are the quintessential city home. Riding the wave of the "creative class" means bringing loft-style condos to the suburbs. The National Association of Homebuilders even built a "loft-inspired detached single-family home" as its representative "New American Home" at the 2004 International Builders' Show.[5] In Reston Town Center, KSI took the urban village model one step further by wrapping a multistory concrete parking garage with loft condominiums on three sides. In many ways, much of what is happening at the town center and other mixed-use developments harkens back to city life a century or more ago.

MIDTOWN TOWERS: URBAN HOME, URBAN VILLAGER

Even with obvious demand for high-rise condos in northern Virginia, KSI made somewhat of a leap of faith in the depth of the high-end market. Area sales of multifamily condos and co-ops in the price range of $1 million plus have been almost entirely within the District of Columbia, yet research revealed a market expanding into Fairfax County and the neighboring urban districts of Arlington and Alexandria. Furthermore, a dynamic urban culture exists in the town center that parallels that of high-income downtown Washington. Of course, the difference is that Reston Town Center has been wholly built upon the fields of suburban Virginia, while the historic city has evolved over centuries.

Residents will move into the 21-story Midtown East and West towers in Fall 2006. Facing one another with a landscaped pool, courtyard, and club at center, these high-rise residences combine the privacy of a detached home with the amenities of a luxury hotel and spa. Large and open floor plans, spacious balconies, large windows, and high-quality finishes and craftsmanship combine with concierge and valet services, a fitness club, state-of-the-art kitchen and dining room for private parties, and secure underground parking. The towers sold in record time: In the 11 months between May 2004 and April 2005 the town center's newest residents bought over 90 percent, a total of 270 of Midtown's units. Industry analysts initially raised concerns about a marketing strategy with a product valued over 25 percent (per square foot) above the best products previously offered in Reston until the depth and diversity of the market was confirmed. Both Midtown high-rises achieved sales prices well in

RESTON TOWN SQUARE FOUNTAINS.

excess of these early targets—on a par with and above many Georgetown houses in downtown Washington. All of this proves that within northern Virginia, there is a proximate market for the residences at Reston Town Center, backed by buyers' large incomes and expensive tastes.

For developers to compete effectively in mixed-use projects, collaboration between different developers has become necessary. They need to increasingly partner with others who possess complementary skills and adjacent, compatible properties. This is often seen when residential and office developers rely upon each others' strengths and cooperate on project components, such as retail, to create the best retail mix and overall neighborhood context. In fact, the ability to collaborate may be the most prized skill in this climate. Also, with land being so expensive, developers must approach projects imaginatively. They need to think in terms of verticality, density, and transit-related mixed-use. Although vertical development means the challenges of higher construction costs, longer approvals, huge capital requirements, multi-disciplinary staffing, and new development partners, the prospect of the coming innovations is extremely exciting.

Midtown is the final step in Reston Town Center becoming a 24-hour city. Its success demonstrates that the suburbs, including areas comparable to Washington's northern Virginia, need and can sustain urban cores. This town center sets an example to depart from the century-old Euclidean zoning and breathe new life into the suburbs with mixed-use design. Blending a critical mass of density and verticality with green spaces, housing, offices, theaters, restaurants, and shops creates an environment where people, not cars, take precedence. Convenience, safety, amenities, and style: that is what the residents of Reston Town Center wanted, and that is what the Midtown neighborhood offers.

Laura Lewis, a freelance writer based in Washington, D.C., contributed to this chapter.

VISIONS FOR RESTON TOWN CENTER

A DIALOGUE

ROBERT E. SIMON

with RAYMOND A. RITCHEY, ROBERT C. KETTLER, *and* ALAN WARD

Robert Simon, you started planning a town center more than 40 years ago.
Has the town center realized your vision? ALAN WARD

The town center was one of the original ideas for
Reston—five village centers and one urban town
center. ROBERT SIMON

If we were to start all over, we would start
walking down Market Street, the residential
placed here and the commercial there, the
library and hospital down an adjoining street.
I wouldn't think of driving. It would be a
completely walkable community.
ROBERT SIMON

People like Reston Town Center because it's a people-watching place, a comfortable place in the scale, sidewalks, stores, and parks. Yet, at this time, the retail mix offers a limited shopping menu; there are no high-end specialty stores and the anchors are vignettes of their larger models. This will change, I think, as the people living here demand more. BOB KETTLER

Market Street is just right; it's a gathering place. ROBERT SIMON

Reston Town Center has achieved significant visibility in the development community. How do you compare it to other projects? ALAN WARD

The growing residential base is accelerating its appeal. BOB KETTLER

Reston Town Center has survived collapses of the economy because it has universal appeal. And, net effective rents at Reston Town Center are some of the highest in the U.S. today, with effectively a zero-percent vacancy. RAY RITCHEY

Reston Town Center established "town center" as a very complimentary term of art.
RAY RITCHEY

I can't see that there is anything, nationally or regionally, that competes with this town center.
ROBERT SIMON

What are key features that are attracting people to buy or lease in
Reston Town Center? ALAN WARD

People who live and work in our suburbs want
to experience an urban environment. Thanks
to Reston Town Center, they don't have to travel
20 miles to downtown Washington to experience
it. The key to the town center's success
is critical mass. RAY RITCHEY

We have found that good architecture and good
planning pay, at least a 15 percent premium.
Reston Town Center has a real community, a
place to eat, drink, live, work, even make out
with your wife at the mailbox if you want. It's
the sense of community... people feel it the
minute they walk in. BOB KETTLER

Reston Town Center is most newsworthy for the sense of community. This is the most valuable asset. When you say "Reston Town Center," you have a vision . . . as a tenant, a resident, a visitor. It's an extremely positive picture of a place.
RAY RITCHEY

People want to live where they work, to live in a creative environment. Our historic cities have evolved the same way. In Reston, people live where they work. That's what they want.
BOB KETTLER

Each block of Reston Town Center is focused on an urban grid of streets and open spaces. How does this compare to other suburban places and to what degree is this part of the success of the town center? ALAN WARD

Our commitment is to see that the streetscape is unified and universal. What we face in the building trade generally is commoditization of office space. We try to achieve just the opposite with each of our buildings: a very special place to experience. RAY RITCHEY

A strong market is half the answer in creating an urban place. Plazas for people are the other half. Reston Town Center does a wonderful job in creating a place for people to gather. ROBERT SIMON

The ability to have live, performing art in Reston Town Square will further animate the urban environment. This is also a park where people can gather and enjoy the scene.
BOB KETTLER

The streets at Reston Town Center are privately owned. How does this effect the perception of the town center as a community gathering place? ALAN WARD

The developers of Reston Town Center chose to build private streets to create an urban downtown environment. Otherwise, suburban zoning would have mandated greater setbacks, rather than what we have here . . . buildings lining sidewalks and streetfront shops . . . like a real city. BOB KETTLER

The town center's streets behave as public streets, even though they are private property. As Reston Town Center gains more building owners and an association of residents who own property, it will behave like a public place. RAY RITCHEY

Since Robert Simon's first prescient plans for an urban town center in 1964, a mix of uses has been an integral part of the thinking. Can you comment on the uses that are now part of the town center? ALAN WARD

Reston Town Center is most valued for high density, high quality, mixed use, a downtown in the suburbs. ROBERT SIMON

Institutions and associations created by the residents will take time, just as with all our great cities. RAY RITCHEY

In all that we do, we try to replicate the dynamics
that have been created at Reston Town Center,
a live-work-play environment for residents and
visitors. RAY RITCHEY

You could add a church, a child-care center.
ROBERT SIMON

Washington, D.C. developer Robert Gladstone stated back in 1974 that if you have a good urban design plan, Reston Town Center can absorb mediocre architecture. What are your thoughts? ALAN WARD

See if you can't have a little fun with the design of buildings and public spaces . . . just to be mischievous, the environment is too sober.
ROBERT SIMON

Mass transit was included in the early generation of plans. Will transit come and will it change Reston Town Center?

We should have Metro coming right through the town center. RAY RITCHEY

The way to sell Metro to Congress and the people is to wave the flag. Do not give statistics that are not immune to skepticism. Use patriotism as your only persuasive argument: The U.S. cannot afford to be the only developed nation without light rail in its nation's capital. ROBERT SIMON

The demand for Metrorail will reach a tipping point, and the ability to pay to build it will be a non-issue. BOB KETTLER

Is Reston Town Center a model to emulate in other parts of the country? ALAN WARD

Across the U.S. today, you see one-story shopping centers everywhere . . . everything is spread out. There should be more density, more uses mixed together, like Reston Town Center. ROBERT SIMON

We have to remember that developers, planners, and designers have been nursing Reston Town Center along for over 40 years. BOB KETTLER

We are the beneficiaries of what previous generations of developers have graciously provided for those of us who are building the last vacant parcels of the town center.
RAY RITCHEY

The reality is that people vote with their behavior and their pocket book. Why pay a premium of 15 to 35 percent to live here? It's the environment, the community. People enjoy their life here.
BOB KETTLER

URBAN TASTES AND SUBURBAN LIVING

PHILIP LANGDON

"TOWN CENTER" HAS become a very flexible term. Fifty years ago, if you had heard someone mention a town center, what probably would have come to mind was a *Saturday Evening Post* kind of image: a small place, strung out along one or two streets, where local people ran into one another at the drug store, the hardware store, the cafe or diner, the municipal building, and on the steps of the post office. The town center served all sorts of everyday needs, but rarely did it have tall, imposing buildings. More often it was just the opposite: a modest, down-to-earth place where most merchants owned their businesses and were reluctant to spend much money introducing the latest trends and fashions. Arthur J. Vidich and Joseph Bensman, in their classic *Small Town in Mass Society*, portrayed small-town shopkeepers in the 1950s as individuals trapped in a "psychology of scarcity-mindedness," afraid to modernize with any flair, because they had only a small pool of potential customers and they sensed that sizable investments would not pay off.

Does this sound like Reston Town Center? Not in the least. Where the old town centers were low to the ground, Reston's is tall. Where old town centers were intensely local and suffused with frugality, Reston's is affluent and designed to attract a mobile, metropolitan population. Where old town centers had little need for office buildings, Reston's is a hive of corporate activity. Yet Reston Town Center does have some of the same physical traits that made provincial town centers appealing. You can walk *on sidewalks* from one end to the other in less than five minutes; though we live in a time of sprawl, Reston's center is geographically contained. The buildings come right up to the narrow streets and sidewalks where people congregate, helping to make the outdoor areas well-defined and coherent. Like the old town centers—and unlike much

OPPOSITE
RESTAURANT DINING
OPENS ONTO THE
PLAZA.

of what Americans build today—Reston Town Center accommodates a variety of activities, and consequently comes to life in a way that an office park or strip shopping center does not. Reston Town Center feels like a *place*.

People have debated whether "town center" is the right term for what is being created in Reston. The best answer to this question is that the name reflects Reston's socially progressive origins. It was a "new town," one of the premier American specimens of a community planning movement that inspired widespread enthusiasm during the 1960s. Robert E. Simon envisioned a community where people of varied incomes could live in a pleasing landscape, nurture ties to their fellow residents, and at the same time enjoy all the benefits of a great metropolis. For everyday shopping and gathering, each of Reston's five sections was laid out with a "village center," beginning with the European-

THE URBANIZATION
OF RESTON TOWN
CENTER.

influenced Lake Anne. The crowning achievement was to be the town center. It would serve people from throughout Reston's rolling seven thousand acres.

During the years that planning for Reston Town Center remained on the back burner—the new town needed to develop and fill with people before the town center would be feasible—other developers, many of them in places less populous than Reston, picked up the idea of town center—meaning a sociable, open-air, pedestrian-scaled, predominantly commercial development. They helped to make it a national phenomenon. An example was the transformation of a one-dimensional strip shopping center into Mashpee Commons, beginning in the mid-1980s. Developers Arnold B. Chace and Douglas Storrs added to that ordinary Cape Cod strip center a grid of narrow streets where traffic moved slowly and pedestrians felt at ease. Within the grid they constructed stores opening onto the sidewalks rather than onto the typical barren parking lots. Chace and Storrs created a compact, walkable precinct that offered stores, eating and drinking places, a post office, and a small number of offices and living quarters. The result: Mashpee Commons resembled the business area of an old small town. As the new urbanism movement gained momentum in the 1990s and in the current decade, many other "town centers" also cropped up around the country. The buildings in these centers usually rose just high enough to give the outdoor spaces a pleasing sense of enclosure and make people feel comfortable.

Nonetheless, most of the town centers constructed since the mid-1980s fall short of Reston's—literally. Many are only two stories high. And though the centers may contain office space, usually the offices are small, accommodating local real estate firms, insurance agencies, lawyers, and doctors but providing no opportunities for organizations that employ hundreds. Missing, in most cases, are the big, open-floor offices that large companies demand. The center that the Walt Disney Company developed in Celebration, Florida, is a prime example. Celebration Town Center is a lovely place to stroll, with streets and sidewalks that turn here and there to present an interesting succession of vistas. It possesses varied and in some cases extremely clever architecture by

prominent designers; the one-of-a-kind buildings attract attention but do not overwhelm. A relaxing promenade overlooks a lake. What the center at Celebration does not have, though, is large number of people working there, spilling out of office buildings at lunch and through the day. Those buildings where substantial numbers of people earn a living have been separated from the town center and placed in another part of the Disney development—in what is essentially an office park. Perhaps Disney believed that Celebration's magical spell would be broken if residents and tourists rubbed shoulders with people earning their pay.

Reston exhibits ambitions that were atypical for its time. Its first office buildings at Fountain Square rose eleven stories. The next two office building on Market Street rose 16 and 18 stories. The Midtown residential towers will reach still higher, 21 stories. Despite the proliferation of town centers, Reston is a rarity. It is a town center with a *skyline*.

Reston is also distinguished by its choice of style. Centers in the past 20 years have mostly tended to project an old-fashioned, cozy appearance. They do not look like serious workplaces for a corporate age. Reston, by contrast, is fully in tune with the corporate economy. When asked why they are attracted to Reston Town Center, businesses cite several factors. Among the most important: the location in a Fairfax County corridor containing numerous other high-tech companies; proximity to Dulles International Airport five miles west; ease of access along the Dulles Toll Road and other major roads; the convenience of being able to walk to restaurants and stores; and the inviting atmosphere. Dense concentrations of housing have been built around the town center's periphery and an impressive number of handsome condominiums and rental apartment buildings have recently been built a block from the center's core, within a pleasant walk of the offices, stores, and restaurants. Much more housing within and near the town center is in the works or planned for construction within the decade. And while only a fraction of those who work in the town center will ever live here, the influx of residents should give the town center added depth.

OPPOSITE LEFT
RESTON TOWN
CENTER FOUNTAIN
SQUARE PLAZA DUR-
ING A SPECIAL EVENT
AND A BEAUTIFUL
DAY IN EARLY
SPRING.

OPPOSITE RIGHT
EARLY EVENING
ON MARKET STREET,
LOOKING WEST
TOWARD FREEDOM
SQUARE.

LEFT
WELL-DESIGNED SIGNAGE ADDS CHARACTER TO TOWN CENTER STREETS.

RIGHT
PLAYING AROUND THE FOUNTAIN

LEFT
PEDESTRIAN BRIDGE FROM RESTON TOWN CENTER TO DISCOVERY SQUARE AND RESTON OVERLOOK.

RIGHT
PANERA BREAD SHOP OPENS OUT TO THE PUBLIC PLAZA AND INTO THE LOBBY OF THE HYATT REGENCY RESTON HOTEL.

In his 1991 book, *Edge City*, Joel Garreau noted that many large metropolitan areas have spawned "edge cities"—substantial outlying centers that cater to a variety of uses. Garreau, expanding on earlier work by Christopher Leinberger, defined an edge city as containing five-million or more square feet of office space and 600,000 or more square feet of retail space. Reston Town Center has not yet accumulated as much office and retail space as Garreau prescribed, but it does perform the functions he identified: bringing businesspeople within relatively close range of one another, offering hotels where business travelers and others can spend the night, and providing restaurants and shopping places. If an edge city is, as Garreau claimed, a major activity center located beyond the traditional downtown and achieving a density greater than its suburban surroundings, Reston Town Center seems to fit the classification.

I would argue that Reston Town Center is an edge city that has achieved a higher order than its peers: it is not the circulatory and visual mess embodied by so many other edge cities, such as nearby Tysons Corner, which has office buildings positioned between parking lots, with grass and trees intended to make the view less noxious. It is often impossible to walk comfortably from office buildings to restaurants, shops, and nearby hotels. Instead, people get in their cars and drive only a mile or so for lunch and errands, creating traffic congestion at lunchtime as well as in the morning and late afternoon.

Garreau argued that in time the congested edge cities would get their act together and become well-organized physical environments. For the most part, that has not happened at this time. It is exceedingly difficult to redesign a place whose original infrastructure was badly conceived. "Tysons is the world's biggest traffic jam," said a law firm's administrator with offices at Reston Town Center and other locations in the Washington region. "When at the end of the day you can't get out of your parking lot or your garage at Tysons because of the shoppers, it's frustrating." Evidence of this town center's superiority to conventional edge cities is that some companies occupying large amounts of office space—in some instances even entire buildings—have recently left Tysons Corner for Reston Town Center. They flee a chaotic environment for a place that is more comfortable and efficient.

Baltimore-based retail consultant Seth Harry explained that rents in the town center "now enjoy a premium over Tysons Corner, the previous office rent king in northern Virginia." In December 2002, for example, SI International, an information technology firm, moved its corporate headquarters from Tysons to a corporate campus just across a footbridge from the town center. Most of SI's 220 employees "have a shorter and less time-consuming commute" than before, and "thoroughly enjoy the ability to take a short walk over the bridge to eat or shop in the town center," said vice president Steve Hunt, who was responsible for choosing the location. "The town center is a great place to meet customers or co-workers without having to get in the car (as was essential in Tysons) and fight traffic." In a competitive job market like greater Washington, quality of life is more than a nicety; it has real value for employers and employees alike.

When the town center's owners in the 1990s promoted Reston as northern Virginia's "new downtown," this was something of a misnomer. Downtowns are *public* places. Their streets and sidewalks and many, though not all, of their parks and gardens are legal parts of the public realm. In a downtown, people can chant protest slogans, pass out campaign leaflets, and congregate even if their presence annoys property owners, employers, and shoppers. By contrast, the core of Reston Town Center is a privately-owned and privately-managed domain. The owners possess the right—and, with paid security guards, the capacity—to exclude anyone who might threaten the town center's ambience. In this, the town center follows the example of nearly every shopping mall or corporate campus in the United States. Most owners of town centers built in the past two decades have sought to avoid the problems of old downtowns in the public domain by keeping the streets and gathering spaces private. By so doing, the owners maintain a desired atmosphere and protect their investment.

In turn, many cities in recent years have recognized that downtowns must become more orderly and attractive if they are to survive and prosper.

TOP
LOW-DENSITY
DEVELOPMENT SUR-
ROUNDS THE URBAN
CORE ON THE NORTH
AND WEST, LOOKING
SOUTH TOWARD RESTON
TOWN CENTER'S
FREEDOM SQUARE
ONE AND TWO. THE
SURFACE LOT OFFERS
A GRIDDED LAND BANK
TO OWNER EQUITY
OFFICE PROPERTIES.

BOTTOM
SALLIE MAE HEAD-
QUARTERS ON
BLUEMONT PARKWAY,
RESTON TOWN CENTER.

Consequently city governments, property owners, and merchants have collaborated to form business improvement districts in hundreds of downtowns and neighborhoods. Typically the districts hire staff to clean the sidewalks, maintain street plantings, and discourage activities such as panhandling. They often retain marketing and programming professionals to promote and bring special events to the district. Business improvement districts in New York City and elsewhere in the last 20 years have demonstrated that it is possible to maintain order and safety while upholding free speech rights. The owners of the new town centers instead believe that private streets and outdoor spaces are far preferable; they see opening the town center to public control as not worth the risk.

From the start, Reston Town Center has shown that it is possible to achieve a degree of urbanity in a new development, miles away from downtown Washington. Reston's developers integrated a multi-screen cinema into a traditional streetscape, putting theaters above the ground floor—a technique that has since become commonplace from Boston to Albuquerque. The town center's Market Street, proportioned to create a degree of enclosure, and Fountain Square, with its sculpture and water fountain, have proven appealing to people from suburban Fairfax and Loudoun counties, and beyond. People come from a broad region, drawn by an outdoor environment that is well defined, architecturally alluring, and animated—people love to watch and be a part of a busy scene.

The town center's grid is filling in and becoming more dense. Developers of the urban core—Equity Office Properties; KSI Services; and Boston Properties—are already looking to replace one- and two-story structures with much taller buildings. Surface parking lots will sprout high-rise buildings, and the lively, pedestrian-oriented atmosphere will expand. That the transformation to a higher-density environment is happening only fifteen years after Reston Town Center first opened is remarkable; it is a sign that the plan is working.

Beyond the core of the town center Reston becomes truly suburban. Pedestrians who stroll a couple of blocks beyond Market Street find that the

COURTYARD OF THE
SAVOY CONDOMINI-
UMS, DEVELOPED BY
TRAMMELL CROW
RESIDENTIAL,
2003–2004.

dense, traditional city pattern gives way to parking lots, one-story strip centers, a campus-like office landscape, and wide roads that are not very comfortable for pedestrians. The six-lane Reston Parkway with fast-moving traffic separates the easternmost Town Center parcel, where Stratford House stands from the urban core and the Hyatt Hotel and Freedom Plaza open out; the parkway has no crosswalks for pedestrians. Residents of the Stratford and other housing clustered on the east side of the parkway are tantalizingly close to the shops of Market Street, but they avoid walking across the parkway; instead, they get in cars for a half-block drive to the town center. New Dominion Parkway on the north also acts as a barrier to pedestrians who might otherwise walk between the town center and the public library and housing on the other side of the parkway. To the west, Town Center Parkway prevents a sizable residential area from being part of the town center. All this is to say that the traffic engineering standards of the Virginia Department of Transportation (VDOT) limit developers' and planners' ability to extend the walkable environment very far. Traditional new town principles that mandated separating pedestrians from the automobile have been lost at the edge of the town center. VDOT has lagged behind the most progressive state transportation departments in adjusting standards to meet pedestrian and community-design protocols.

One wonders whether all the buildings are as engaging as they might be. The two long blocks of apartment and condominium units built by Trammell Crow at the western edge of the town center, The Savoy, make a strong urban impression with their four-story height and dignified masonry exteriors. Yet the developer of this 700-unit cluster placed just a few entrances on the street. In an ideal urban environment, the blocks would be designed as townhouses or as groups of apartments with scores of entrances along the street, to and from the town center. A series of stairs or stoops similar to those that distinguish the great brownstone and rowhouse neighborhoods of Boston, Chicago, Philadelphia, and San Francisco, among others, or side-by-side front patios, like those insisted upon by planning authorities in downtown Vancouver, British Columbia, would encourage impromptu interaction and personalized street facades. These would enhance the town center's animation. In other buildings at Reston Town Center—around Freedom Square and along Market Street—the developers and designers have devoted great care to make the pedestrian experience fun and stimulating.

Some visitors to Reston Town Center describe the atmosphere as "corporate." What they mean by this, I think, is that the center emanates a businesslike restraint. The center's retailers and restaurants, predominantly medium-priced to high-end national chains, in combination with the dignified architecture, generate a mainstream and affluent flavor. Some urbanist thinkers, from Jane Jacobs to Leon Krier, argue that a genuinely urban place offers a tremendous variety. The best cities have room for enterprise and individuals that span the economic and societal spectrum. This variety allows individuals with all sorts of interests and backgrounds to explore and express their own nature, as idiosyncratic as that may be. Ideally, an urban setting enables individuals to make intellectual, emotional, and spiritual connections—which is why so many artists, thinkers, and creative people have for centuries gravitated to cities. In the long run, flexibility and variety make a city strong.

It may seem out of place to apply such a distinctly urban standard to a town center in the middle of the suburbs. But suburbs are rapidly changing and diversifying. During the great wave of suburbanization that occurred after World War II, outlying towns functioned mostly as bedroom communities, catering to the needs of young families with children at home—families looking for freestanding houses with ample yards. During the past quarter-century, however, the population and activities of the suburbs have grown and broadened, making that single-minded focus on family life something of the past. By 1994, according to Brookings Institution, more Americans lived in the suburbs than anywhere else, and in coming years outlying communities will continue to capture the majority of new residents and new jobs. The suburban reality in the 21st century is diversity—in population, employment, and style of life.

"Suburbs now contain more nonfamily households—largely young singles and elderly people living alone—than married couples with children," William H. Frey and Alan Berube reported in a Brookings analysis of the 2000 U. S. Census. Americans in general have gravitated toward more urban tastes in the past twenty years, as can be seen in the rise of Starbucks. Many of these people want to have lively places near their work—ideally, within walking distance—where they can relax or socialize, or eat or drink during the day and into the night. All of this leads to demand for higher-density housing and inter-mixing of residences, workplaces, retail, and entertainment. That Reston Town Center's developers anticipated and responded to key economic and demographic trends is a fact that will be with us for many years to come.

The town center has shown that a concentration of diverse activities can thrive in suburbia, especially in a metropolitan area that is large and relatively cosmopolitan. Reston has brought to the Washington region a handsome, and in many ways appealing, reinterpretation of traditional urban elements. It has shown that open-air sidewalks do attract people, in winter and in summer. It has demonstrated that a large number of businesses, employees, and recently-

arrived residents prefer pedestrian-scaled, mixed-use surroundings and are willing to pay a premium to be there. They willingly (and ably) pay for this value-added increment in rents, condominium prices, and restaurant tabs. Reston has reintegrated important parts of daily life. As the town center's population grows, so will the opportunities for adding to, and deepening, the center's dimensions. Reston Town Center has become a favorite site for community fairs, festivals, fund-raisers, concerts, and parades. It is a place where people want to spend time, for many different purposes and in many different times of the day or week. The experiment in town-making is succeeding as a cultural, artistic, and economic phenomenon, pioneering a path from which many other suburbs could learn.

A BROOKLYN BOY IN RESTON TOWN CENTER

THERE SHOULD BE MORE PLACES LIKE THIS

TOM VANDERBILT

THE SCENE IS an American city in December. In the town's Fountain Square, a gaily-festooned fir commands pride of place, while the streets sparkle with lights and ornaments. Banners strung across streetlamps announce next weekend's holiday parade. Evening shoppers consider gifts at the Williams-Sonoma store, or stop to study the movie posters beneath the theater's art-deco neon sign. Taxis trawl by as smartly dressed office workers, still wearing badges from Accenture or one of the other downtown firms, pause on corners to check their Blackberrys and answer cell phones. Groups of diners wait for a table outside Clyde's of Georgetown, a popular redoubt of American classic cooking, or perhaps they are already tucking into the mango chicken at the Indonesian restaurant just down the block.

The heart of activity tonight is centered around the downtown's outdoor skating rink, bustling with groups out for an evening's glide across the ice: There is a group of Asian teenagers who skate four abreast, jostling and laughing; the Latino couple gliding arm-and-arm, wearing matching Dolce & Gabbana sweatshirts; a particularly agile skater propels himself backwards and banks away from the walls at alarmingly late moments, to the delight of three women who have stopped to watch.

To the experienced connoisseur of urban experiences, there are recognizable signifiers here—walkable streets, tall buildings, even the snatches of overheard conversation—that read within our systems of environmental awareness as *urban* things. Taking a few memorable parts on a first glance—the soaring Christmas tree, the skating rink, the rain-slicked streets reflecting the glow of the theater—one thinks this could be Rockefeller Center, or at least it seems to contain certain strands of its DNA. Keep walking a few blocks, how-

OPPOSITE
SKATERS WHIRL
AROUND THE
PAVILION RINK IN
FOUNTAIN SQUARE
PLAZA.

ever, and you might experience, as the popular movie series had it, a "glitch in the matrix"; a geographic disconnect where suddenly the urbanity gives way to a massive parking lot, or a cluster of mid-rise office parks sitting astride a highway. Your compass starts to spin.

But that is the frontier. Stay in the center of this place and you feel as if you are in a familiar place, now revealed to be Reston Town Center, a place that makes sense to the pedestrian consciousness. In the sprawl-and-highway, hub-and-spoke landscape of northern Virginia you feel as if you had suddenly arrived at a kind of oasis, where you can find food, drink, shops, and perhaps a place to sit for a moment and take a contemplative rest. There is something reassuring about the monumentality of Fountain Square, the pomp of the shining bronze Mercury statue and the surrounding high-rise architecture; one realizes that it feels good to inhabit a place that has a *sense of place*.

I admit that I am betraying a bias here—as a resident of Brooklyn, New York, a place in which urbanism is the only option, in which whatever questions about how its scale or function or circulation were mostly answered long ago, in which I partake in a "modern lifestyle" that yet somehow seems antiquated in many other parts of the country (I meet friends at a hipster bar a block away; I walk to buy my dinner from a butcher and a fish monger; I do not drive to work). Massive discount clubs, office parks, and gated golf communities leave me deeply cold. Which is why I had to come to Reston Town Center with a certain reflective skepticism. In the cab on the way to Reston, I thought, was this just not another featureless edge city? To my surprise, I found that my senses—usually all out of whack in the suburbs—quite easily and naturally grew accustomed to the streets of the town center. Instead of suburban vertigo, I noticed I was walking, and behaving, rather instinctively in a place that felt familiar, designed more for people than cars.

The skating rink provides a clue to what is going on here. An implicit attraction of city life is the ability to be both performer and voyeur, to see and be seen. Urban life, as has been observed before, is a kind of stage set. One does not generally find street musicians or fashionable dandies or even end-of-times

OPPOSITE, CLOCKWISE
FROM TOP LEFT
PLACE MARKERS IN
TOWN CENTER.

THE GIANT
CHRISTMAS TREE
WITH THE MERCURY
FOUNTAIN.

MEETING PEOPLE
ON THE STREET.

SKATER ON THE
PAVILION RINK

ranters on leafy suburban streets, for they need an audience of appreciable mass. For the skaters at Reston Town Center, there are certainly all sorts of other ways they could have chosen to pass their time: they could have rented DVDs to take home and watched them in private. These people, however, wanted to see things, to be in the company of other people, perhaps to become players in an uncontrolled minor drama that is always changing, and yet it is always a bit familiar.

In the past, this kind of experience would have required traveling 20 miles into downtown Washington; or perhaps journeying to an enclosed shopping mall, a placebo place that somehow seems one-dimensional and ordered, for any real dramatic satisfaction. They have come, instead, to a place that is emerging as something of a model for what the twenty-first century will look like, how it will perform, and what functions it will serve.

It seems fitting that this new place should be Reston, for no other American new town of the 1960s captured as much attention as the model

RESTON TOWN CENTER'S MASS TRANSIT. METRORAIL TO COME.

community envisioned by Robert E. Simon. Reston, unlike what was to come in the American suburban landscape, was intensively planned—down to the proprietary cable television system Simon installed so that antennas would not blight the landscape. Reston did not evolve exactly as Simon scripted it over four decades ago—there was never the bridle path into town so the equestrian Restonian could "could leave his horse and enter the Town Center directly"— and its various financial troubles in the 1970s and 1980s were indicative in part of its sheer ahead-of-itself-ness. One is struck even today to travel to Lake Anne Plaza, the model of 1960s new town urbanism, and sit with a cup of coffee and take in a landscape that you will find nowhere else in America— European coastal enclave meets Scandinavian modernism.

Reston began life at a time when the city in America was in absolute retreat, experiencing outright urban flight. In anchoring his new town with village centers, and eventually, Simon hoped, a complete "urban core," Simon was articulating a countervailing trend to what was actually happening. He was reinstalling a romantic vision of what Main Street could be, in much the same spirit, if not the letter, as Walt Disney. For what were all those legions of people who first visited Disneyland and Disneyworld in the 1960s and 1970s doing if not experiencing the wonders of town life that was increasingly absent in their own suburban existences, as well as witnessing a vision of what could be—idealized Tomorrowlands with clean and quite monorails where the trash was magically whisked away? Disney creators found after decades of research that what brought people to the parks was not the rides and spectacles but the overall environment. Architect and urbanist Charles Moore, in his influential essay "You Have to Pay for the Public Life," described an ethos that might apply equally to Simon as to Disney: "it occurs to some, as the gray domestic waves of suburban sea fill in the valleys and the bays, and lap at and erode the hills, that something should be done, and that the something should be urban and monumental.... but even more basic than the absence of a viable architectural idiom for making public centers is the absence of any establishment ready to shoulder the responsibility for, to take a proprietary interest in, the public realm." The establishment was clearly not ready for a pioneering development like Reston; indeed, when first planned, it was illegal.

Reston was always intended to have a center to it, a place that as Simon described was "to be like a city, rather than the sterility of a glass-enclosed shopping mall," a place that would anchor the constellation of developments. Time and circumstances, however, conspired against it. First, Reston's villages had to acquire enough population to sustain a town center; second, much of the commercial development that did go on was directed toward other places. By the 1980s, the time had arrived: the people had come and businesses lined the twenty-mile highway between D.C. and Dulles Airport. The process of planning Reston Town Center began. This was a watershed moment in American town development.

Where cities had historically evolved organically owing to a geographically strategic location, and then seen rail-linked garden suburbs and car-dependent subdivisions spin off from there, typically over the course of many decades, Reston had begun as essentially a series of suburbs that, several decades later, was now looking for a center. It was inside-out urbanism. "We're filling the hole in the doughnut," said an architect with RTKL, Reston Town Center's designers. This was city-making from scratch—rather than dealing with historic districts or old infrastructural networks, Reston Town Center was a city of the imagination, of the future. *The New York Times* predicted that Reston was "setting a new national pattern for what would be called a new city." In just one measure of how speculative it all was, the name of Reston's spiritual downtown was not even certain, and advertising companies polled residents to gauge reactions to choices that included "Reston City" and "The City At Reston."

It might strike some as exceedingly artificial that a city should be devised out of thin air, on virgin dirt, after the fact, but this is precisely why Reston Town Center can be seen as a prototype. Mobility and telecommunications, among other things, mean that new cities are not necessarily formed along the lines of old ones; absent the economic imperative or old-style transportation networks or geographical constraints that kept cities tightly ordered, the new American landscape has been proceeding formlessly, so abstract that we are not even sure what to call it. In his book *On Paradise Drive*, a field guide to the exurban landscape, the social commentator David Brooks notes the various terms social scientists have conjured to describe these new regions: "edgeless city, major diversified center, multicentered net, ruraburbia, boomburg, spread city, technoburb, suburban growth corridor, sprinkler cities." In Brooks' reckoning, "Americans move so much and so feverishly that they change the landscape of reality more quickly than we can adjust our mental categories." There is a new exurban reality, Brooks contends: "We have a huge mass of people who not only don't live in the cities, they don't commute to the cities, go to movies in the cities, eat in the cities, or have any significant contact with urban life. They are neither rural, nor urban, nor residents of a bedroom community. They are charting a new way of living."

What is now becoming apparent, however, after several decades of exurban experimentation, is that people still desire density; they want not simply the quantitative benefits that a city can bestow—the creativity and productivity spawned by clustering—but they are longing for the qualitative aspects of urban life. They want to be able to stroll aimlessly, to go from store to restaurant without another perilous commute, to visit an art gallery and then sit at an outdoor café, and, as in Reston, to pause for a moment to watch something as simple as skaters enjoying a winter's night. They want convenience, but also community—as Brooks says, they want "Mayberry with Blackberrys." It is striking that within the last decade, in addition to Reston, some of the most significant new towns in the world—England's Milton Keynes and the Dutch satellite city of Almere, places also built in the 1960s away from city centers—have [only lately] been reinserting their own swatches of urban fabric. "The original planners were smart enough to say, 'We could build it now and build it mediocre, or we can simply wait until there's enough pressure to allow for something really high quality,'" explained an architect with Rem Koolhaas' Office for Metropolitan Architecture, the firm responsible for planning Almere's new city center.

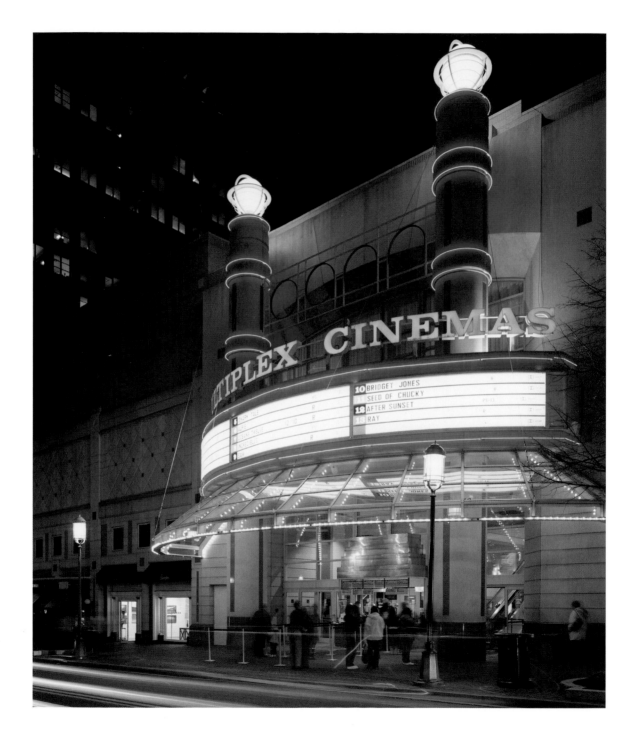

Similarly, it was arguably propitious that Reston's builders and planners took longer than expected for the town center to come to fruition. In doing so some of the planning mistakes of previous decades were avoided: a 1970s scheme for the town center, for example, was a modernist shopping center on steroids. By the time planning began, it was becoming apparent that people in essence wanted a return to classic urbanism: civic spaces, a mixture of residential and commercial, human-scaled streets, and the occasion for spontaneity.

Now, a very curious thing is happening. Real estate values are beginning to rise, even eclipsing traditional exurban locales such as Tysons Corner, the epitome of the 1980s "edge city." There is in fact a kind of "exurban flight" from places like Tysons to Reston, as people tire of haphazard sprawl and worsening traffic congestion. "We pretty much think Reston is becoming the center of the area and we want to be here," the CEO of a technology company told *The Washington Post*. "Tysons Corner just happened over time, where Reston was always master planned.... [Y]ou can tell the difference in the morning and evening drive." This [heightened] interest in Reston's town center is prompting new building plans that supercede the density that was once thought economically sustainable. Where a sprawling parking lot now stands, soon will sprout more shops and offices, and even a park. Where Reston Town Center has been an incipient city—the hopeful idea of a city for a centerless region—it is now beginning to take actual steps toward becoming a real city.

The most tangible display of this can be seen in the 21-story Midtown residential development at the opposite end of Market Street from the earlier Fountain Square. While there is no "midtown" neighborhood to speak of in Reston Town Center, Midtown does rather speak to a certain ideal of urban high-rise living, with its grand lobbies, concierge service, doormen, and expansive views, all of which one might find in Chicago or New York. But not, previously, could they find it in the Northern Virginia suburbs. Midtown is in fact a bit of a conceptual leap, the same way Reston Town Center itself was. As a place, Midtown plays with the perceived categories. We are used to "downtown" being the center of a city, but what happens when downtown, as much as being any

OPPOSITE
MULTIPLEX CINEMA
IS A POPULAR
TOWN CENTER
DESTINATION.

A BROOKLYN BOY IN RESTON TOWN CENTER   167

geographic center, becomes a state of mind? The early indications are that the model proposed—the rather novel idea of luxury urban high-rise living, outside an area where one might traditionally expect to find it—is proving attractive to buyers and yielding high property values. This is the underlying dynamic of the 21st-century city: urbanism is where you want it to be. Thanks to advanced technology, it can be. It does not have to be built upon the traces of the 19th-century city; it does not have to be at the confluence of rivers. Cities are now dynamic organisms, free of set-in-stone entities. They will rise or fall depending on an enduring truth: people want to be where the action is.

As with other planned communities designed ahead of time with ostensibly every need in mind, some may find a certain sterility in Reston Town Center, a sense that its "cityness" calls up images of *The Truman Show*. And indeed, as the town center becomes a real urban place, it has lessons to learn. For example, signs advising that there is "No Trespassing" or "No Loitering" seem more suited to a shopping mall and run counter to the idea of a public realm. Successful urban spaces such as New York City's Bryant Park need order and rules to create a certain comfort level among their users, but they also need to foster openness and a sense of possibility: indeed, "loitering" is the very essence of the pleasures to be found in a place like Bryant Park. But as cities go, Reston is still in its birth stages; we forget that the great cities of America, Chicago and New York, for example, were in the beginning denounced as provincial cow-towns, pale shadows of places like Paris or London. As it evolves, Reston Town Center will gradually assume its own identity, it will figure out what works and what does not, it will acquire history and legend. Reston Town Center is a new urban form for an age whose forms are still taking shape. It is also ingrained with a classic American tradition, the dream of building a better life in a new place.

OPPOSITE

AN URBAN SCENE IN
FOUNTAIN SQUARE.

DESIGNING THE
SUBURBAN CITY

ROBERT A. M. STERN

Blanc 10/'05

AT ITS BEST the American suburban town is a remarkable achievement, not a degraded form of city planning as so many have recently come to argue. The tradition of planned suburbs, and planned town centers within them, flourished in the days that required bedroom communities to be organized around walkable distances and commuter mass transportation, a time before the automobile. These new towns of the railroad era were essentially villages, with curving tree-lined roads and tended lawns that communicated the nearness of the countryside, weaving public and semiprivate open space through the private realm. Usually a rail station provided the focus, as at Frederick Law Olmsted and Calvert Vaux's Riverside, Illinois (1869), the first planned suburb, where a hotel and a commercial block of retail stores and second-floor offices constituted "the downtown."

Sometimes, as a result of their convenient location close to the city by way of railroads, small country towns evolved into suburban cities. Like the planned suburban villages of Riverside or Bronxville, New York, but much bigger, the new suburban cities—such as White Plains, New York; Stamford, Connecticut; or Evanston, Illinois—flourished in the railroad era. But after World War II, parking demands of automobiles swamped them under. Moreover, average Americans as well as affluent ones would entertain only the single-family house on a large plot of land as a desirable place to live. As a result, planners and the country's culture generally got caught up in the liberating effects of the automobile that spawned the sprawling subdivisions that still proliferate.

What's wrong with these sprawling subdivisions? In essence they are non-places. They segregate development by housing type and economic profile, and divorce functions from one another so that there are no centers to

RESIDENTIAL
BUILDINGS
BY STERN.

TOP
AERIAL VIEW FROM
THE SAVOY, LOOKING
SOUTHEAST.

BOTTOM
VIEW FROM
EXPLORER STREET
AND RESTON TOWN
SQUARE.

RENDERINGS BY
ERNEST BURDEN III.

bring neighborhoods together. Instead of building tightly planned Main Streets where civic structures, shops, offices, and in-town housing coalesce, by adopting the model of suburban sprawl Americans embraced the seeming endlessness of the open road and the commercial strip.

Reston Town Center is a long overdue and highly welcome attempt to break the hammerlock hold of sprawl. It belongs to the tradition of suburban urbanism, like White Plains and Evanston, yet it is planned with the car in mind. It is dense in scale and complex in its mix of uses. Its origins lie not in a *de novo* approach to planning but in an evolutionary one.

Robert E. Simon's initial proposal for Reston and its town center was one of the first significant protests against the bleak landscape of suburban sprawl. Though spread out in ways that Olmsted and his disciples would have deemed profligate with the land, Simon's original concept for Reston nonetheless preserved woodlands and wetlands that ran through the site. As importantly, Reston's Lake Anne Village Center in the mid-1960s made a bold stab toward recapturing the idea of the suburban village. It didn't quite work; it wasn't dense enough and it didn't connect to other neighborhoods and mass transit. But it did suggest in its form the idea of a suburban village or town, an idea that had been ignored for a generation.

Today's Reston Town Center succeeds as a city center by bearing witness to a genuine renewal of interest in urbanity. It's a pleasure to be able to experience its dense mix of commercial and residential development along city streets that invite office workers and residents alike to frequent shops and restaurants. The town center plan of blocks and lots, and the guidelines that regulate heights and coverage, all conspire to make good urban architecture possible. The architect's job is to interpret them in relationship to a client's specific requirements, to shape the masses and model the details to provide lively silhouettes and visually engaging surfaces. This is not so easy as it seems; the car is still with us, demanding huge areas for garages.

In our work at Reston Town Center, we have placed as many cars below grade as was feasible and camouflaged the rest behind storefronts that line the sidewalks and maisonettes with stoops and street entries. Our scheme for the block bounded by Town Square, Explorer Street, St. Francis Street, and Bluemont Way takes full advantage of its location on Reston Town Square, with a tower rising to a distinctive crown of duplex apartments marking the corner. An attended entry with a sparkling bronze and glass canopy faces the park, and shops and a restaurant invite pedestrians to stroll along its frontage. The building steps down to the south and west, opening the interior courtyard and garden to sunsets and views to the Blue Ridge Mountains. The other street frontages are lined with sidewalk apartment stoops that enliven the streetscape and emphasize individuality.

At the end of Democracy Drive, a grand portal invites pedestrians to wander through the courtyard, animated by a splashing fountain and garden lushly planted and lined with benches for visitors to linger. A variety of amenities—a health club, a pool deck and spa, community rooms for residents—open directly onto the garden. Tucked around the edges are private patios for the surrounding garden apartments. A stairway at the southwest corner allows the casual visitor or shortcut-taker to return to the sidewalk at Bluemont Way.

Setback massing provides opportunities for rooftop terraces. A mix of apartments including street-level maisonettes, garden-front flats, park-facing lofts, deluxe floor-through flats with private elevator access, and luxury penthouse duplexes accommodates a wide range of residents. In keeping with the predominant character of Reston Town Center, the moderne-inspired buildings are faced with a combination of brick, cast stone, and limestone and articulated with two different types of balconies—some masonry parapets and others delicate metalwork railings—further contributing visual variety and scale to the overall composition.

Across the street at the block bounded by Explorer Street, Democracy Drive, Bluemont Way, and Library Street, the high-density development again accommodates a mix of uses. Streetfront shops step up along the sloping frontage of Democracy Drive, and in the center of the block, a large public garage screened behind a varied facade of brick and cast stone provides 600

parking spaces for shoppers and workers from office buildings across the street. At each end of the block an apartment building wraps the corner, and together they enclose a courtyard roof garden for the use of residents that is set atop the public garage.

At Reston Town Center, we have returned to the time-honored examples of the design of cities—such as wrapping apartment buildings around garden courtyards. In this, we embrace a hierarchy of clearly defined public, semipublic, and private outdoor spaces that are each conceived as specific places—as rooms linked to axes of circulation and view, rooms that participate in the larger network of streets and pedestrian ways that form the arteries of the town center.

TOWARD AN
ORGANIC MODEL FOR CITIES

DESIGN PRINCIPLES FOR A NEW DOWNTOWN

ALAN WARD

THE IDEA OF creating a new town like Reston was, to a degree, a utopian goal. Plans initiated by Robert E. Simon and carried forward by others aimed to create a new American model for residential development. This new American approach ideally would preserve generous corridors of green space sensitive to environmental concerns while building housing for a growing population—the best of both worlds. Conklin & Rossant's design for the early Lake Anne Village Center at Reston was highly calculated, quite beautiful yet rigid. Architect William Conklin acknowledged this in *American Architecture Now* II: "One unsuccessful aspect of Reston was its inability to expand rapidly and yet remain coherent.... We designed a complete model of a town center... but it doesn't grow successfully.... Perhaps the problem all cities face is that of growth and change."

The inability to accommodate change, which is often the failing of utopian visions, has been overcome at Reston Town Center by the flexibility inherent in the block pattern, a classic form of organizing cities. Once the town center is built out by 2010, it will be possible to respond to new demands of the marketplace and redevelop property as required, block by block. In this way, as the town center adapts to changing demands and needs it will more closely resemble downtowns that have evolved over centuries. It will progressively evolve due to pressures of the marketplace, cultural and social needs, and other factors, rather than a predetermined master plan.

As Reston Town Center nears completion, six principles that have guided its development are worth citing. These are fundamental concepts for American urban development, guidelines that might be considered when planning other large-scale mixed-use projects.

THE DESIGN AND SCALE OF FOUNTAIN SQUARE PLAZA HAVE THE RIGHT FEEL AND A SENSE OF URBAN VITALITY.

ROBERT E. SIMON,
FOUNDER OF
RESTON, VIRGINIA.

Start with a vision or "big idea." The master developer was crucial at
Reston Town Center, as were visionaries who had a view of the long-term
"big picture."

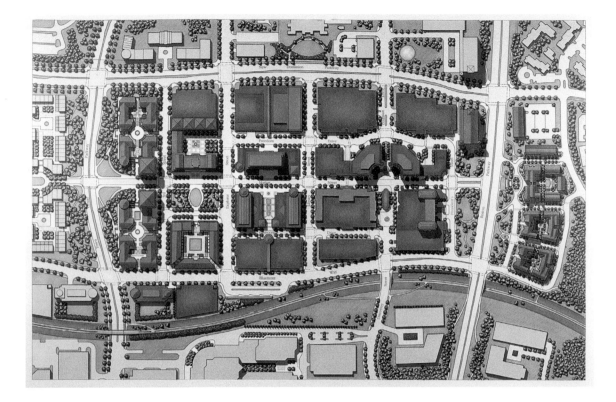

RTKL AND SASAKI
MASTER PLAN, 1990,
FEATURES THE OPEN-
ENDED GRID.

Develop a clear framework of streets and public spaces that enables
development to respond to the market with flexibility.

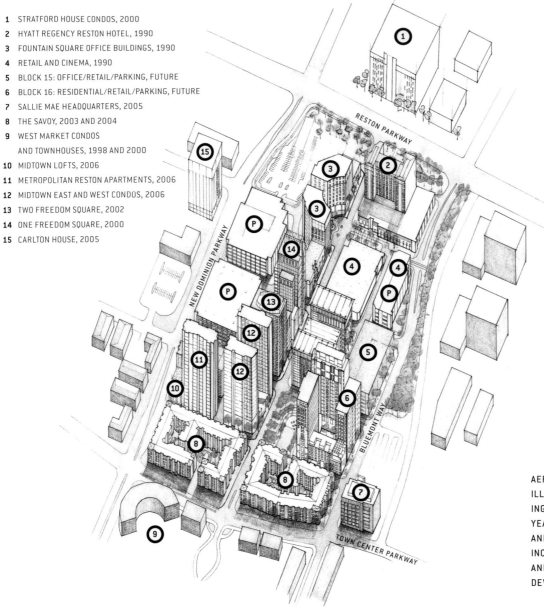

1 STRATFORD HOUSE CONDOS, 2000
2 HYATT REGENCY RESTON HOTEL, 1990
3 FOUNTAIN SQUARE OFFICE BUILDINGS, 1990
4 RETAIL AND CINEMA, 1990
5 BLOCK 15: OFFICE/RETAIL/PARKING, FUTURE
6 BLOCK 16: RESIDENTIAL/RETAIL/PARKING, FUTURE
7 SALLIE MAE HEADQUARTERS, 2005
8 THE SAVOY, 2003 AND 2004
9 WEST MARKET CONDOS
   AND TOWNHOUSES, 1998 AND 2000
10 MIDTOWN LOFTS, 2006
11 METROPOLITAN RESTON APARTMENTS, 2006
12 MIDTOWN EAST AND WEST CONDOS, 2006
13 TWO FREEDOM SQUARE, 2002
14 ONE FREEDOM SQUARE, 2000
15 CARLTON HOUSE, 2005

AERIAL PERSPECTIVE
ILLUSTRATES BUILD-
ING SIZES AND THE
YEAR COMPLETED,
AND HIGHLIHTS THE
INCREASED DENSITY
AND HEIGHT OF LATER
DEVELOPMENT.

Have a long-term commitment to the downtown's development and wait
for the market to support higher densities and a mix of uses—office,
retail, residential, hotel, recreational, and institutional. To build downtown
densities may require the staying power and financial resources of very
large developers.

MARKET STREET,
LOOKING EAST.

4 Leverage real estate value by extending the open-ended grid, which enables later phases to leverage the value of earlier, established phases.

FOUNTAIN SQUARE
PLAZA.

5 Be conscious of the scale of every street, space, plaza, and park during design. It is crucial to create the right feel. A sense of urban vitality is magnified with a plan that achieves an appropriate scale for the pedestrian, and dissipated when spaces are over-scaled, too open, and underused.

ATTENTION TO
DESIGN DETAILS.

6 Design matters. Have a concern for details, but do not be obsessive. A design too mannered and controlled can begin to look fake or contrived. Draw connections between buildings by making relationships of scale and height, along with design treatments, such as cornice lines, building materials, and colors.

CHRONOLOGY OF RESTON TOWN CENTER
PLANNING, DESIGN, DEVELOPMENT

1961

Robert E. Simon, Jr., acquires 6,750 acres in Fairfax County, Virginia, the land upon which the new town of Reston, Virginia, will be built.

1963

Gulf Oil, Inc., buys a substantial interest in Reston, which allows Bob Simon to begin construction of the new town.

1964

Preliminary programming studies of Reston Town Center are completed by Whittlesey & Conklin.

First public discussion of apartments in Reston Town Center.

1965

Lake Anne Village Center officially opens to national acclaim for the innovative plan and architectural design.

Two homeowners' associations (later combined into one) are created to oversee land use and development programming.

Reston Planned Community (RPC) zoning designates the "Town Center Zone" on May 20.

Washington, D.C.–based developer Donahoe & Co. describes plans for the first office building in Town Center for the U. S. General Services Administration, in July.

1967

Gulf Oil creates the subsidiary Gulf Reston, Inc, and takes over planning, construction, financing, and sales of the new town according to the original master plan. Gulf Reston is headed by Robert Ryan. Gulf Reston takes over full financial and operational responsibility of Reston, Virginia on September 28.

The Reston Community Association (RCA) is formed as an independent organization; its principal mission is to keep a watchful eye on the new developer.

1968

Reston Commuter Bus System begins customized service and gains national attention.

1969

Robert Ryan leaves Gulf Reston in April. William Magness, a Gulf Oil executive, becomes chief operations officer of Gulf Reston.

CBS Morning News televises the Reston Commuter Bus story on August 29.

The *Reston Times* begins weekly circulation on October 21.

1972

Gulf Reston's prepaid taxes finance the building of ramps onto the Dulles Access Road, twelve years in advance of the local-access Dulles Toll Road.

Common Ground Foundation begins intra-Reston bus service, forerunner of Reston Internal Bus System (RIBS).

Francis C. Steinbauer is appointed vice president of planning, engineering, and design for Gulf Reston in June.

1973

The RCA and Gulf Reston appear at the Fairfax County Planning Commission in support of a low-density rezoning of the 624-acre southern portion of Reston in January.

Gulf Reston files suit against Fairfax County for sewer taps to serve new construction on January 10.

James Todd is named executive vice president of Gulf Reston in June.

Dulles Express Bus lanes are opened to traffic on July 31.

1974

William Magness appoints James Todd president and chief operating officer of Gulf Reston.

Gulf Reston wins a lawsuit against Fairfax County's sewer hookup moratorium in June.

Gulf Reston Chairman William Magness tells the annual meeting of the Fairfax County Chamber of Commerce that the Board of Supervisors' "slow-growth" and "no-growth" policies have virtually spelled doom for the new town of Reston, in June.

Gulf Reston vs. Fairfax County Board of Supervisors suit is settled, for the plaintiff on October 22.

Greater Reston Arts Center (GRACE) is founded with the mission of enriching community life by promoting involvement and excellence in the visual arts.

1975

The U. S. Department of Housing and Urban Development announces the end of its new town development program in the United States in January.

1977

Gulf Oil, to concentrate on the core business of energy, decides to divests of all income-producing real estate holdings, including Reston, and places all properties on the market.

1978

The Mobil Oil Corporation purchases 3,700 acres of undeveloped land in Reston in July. Mobil Land Development Corporation forms the subsidiary, Reston Land Corporation, and appoints Jim Todd president.

The Fairfax County Board of Supervisors changes the RPC ordinance to Planned Residential Community (PRC) with the adoption of a new zoning ordinance on June 12.

1979

Mobil subsidiary, Reston Land Corporation, buys the Town of Reston, containing 30,000 residents and 349 businesses.

Dulles Access Road parallel toll lanes—to become the Dulles Toll Road—are approved by the Virginia General Assembly. With the approval of the Federal Aviation Administration, owner of the Dulles International Airport, the road is opened to four-person carpools during rush hour in January.

1980

Gulf Reston Inc. sells its income-producing properties to Donatelli and Klein, Inc.; Mark Winkler Management Inc.; and Stephen Yeonas in February.

1981

The Fairfax County Parkway (outer beltway) is discussed in the Fall in an effort to create an acceptable plan for a new cross-country arterial road intersecting or abutting Reston.

The *Reston-Fairfax West Connection*, with Paul Clancy as publisher and Tom Brubisich as editor, begins publication as a bi-weekly newspaper on October 14. Weekly production begins in December.

1982

Reston board of commerce organizes.

Virginia State Highway Commission gives final approval of the Dulles Toll Road on December 16.

1983

Ground-breaking for the Dulles Toll Road in January.

The Dulles connector highway between Route 66 and the Dulles Access Road is opened in December.

1984

The Dulles Toll Road opens.

Jim Todd resigns from Reston Land Corporation and James Cleveland is appointed president.

The Planned Community Archives at George Mason University is created to collect Reston's new town development records and those of other planned communities.

1985

Reston Regional Library opens at Reston Town Center.

Reston Land Corporation's development team discusses naming of town center.

1986

The population of Reston exceeds 45,000 people.

The Dulles Corridor's business expansion—much of it in Reston, where over 1,300 firms employ over 24,000—gains national attention.

Plans for the development of Reston Town Center are unveiled on February 18.

Reston Land Corporation informs Fairfax County that it does not want to include low- and mid-income housing in its project alternatives on July 30.

Reston Land Corporation submits the application for rezoning Reston Town Center on September 25.

1987

Reston Homeowners Association is renamed Reston Association on January 22.

Fairfax Country Planning Commission approves plans for Reston Town Center plans on February 11.

Reston Town Center rezoning is approved by Reston Community Association and Fairfax County.

Reston Town Center development partnership of Reston Land Corporation and Himmel/MKDG (Miller/Klutznick/Davis/Gray) is announced in May.

1988

Reston Land Corporation breaks ground on the construction of Reston Town Center on June 22.

Architects RTKL Associates selected to design the first phase of Reston Town Center.

1989

The 517-room Hyatt Regency Hotel breaks ground at Reston Town Center in March.

Fountain Square office building opens in November.

Thomas J. D'Alesandro IV joins Mobil Land Development Corporation as executive vice president.

1990

The first phase of Reston Town Center, comprised of 530,000 square feet of office space, 200,000 square feet of stores and restaurants, and an eleven-screen movie theater is hailed for its innovative urban design in a suburban setting.

The LINK traffic management program is launched.

1991

Reston Town Center attracts office tenants despite area-wide recession.

1992

Development and planning of Reston Town Center is halted temporarily due to economic recession.

The American Institute of Architects awards RKTL and Sasaki Associates urban design awards for their architectural and landscape design work, respectively, at Reston Town Center.

1994

The Spectrum at Reston Town Center is approved.

Fairfax County Board of Supervisors approves funds to refurbish Lake Anne Plaza.

Fairfax County enacts many provisions of the citizen-sponsored rewrite of the Residential Planned Community (RPC) ordinance.

1997

Boston Properties, in partnership with Dallas-based Terrabrook, start construction on the second phase of Reston Town Center, two 16-story office buildings totaling 900,000square feet. Oracle and BDM buildings at Reston Parkway and Sunset Hills Roads.

1998

Reston Parkway and Sunset Hills Road are among several major street widenings necessitated by large-scale commercial construction. Town of Reston's employment exceeds 45,000.

2000

National Wildlife Federation certifies the Town of Reston a Community Wildlife Habitat. Employment tops 55,000. The last single-family lots are sold and population exceeds 60,000.

2001

Sept 11th terrorist attacks dominate America and the Washington area. High-technology businesses, many located along the Dulles Toll Road corridor, experience downturn.

2002

American Institute of Certified Planners designates Reston founder Robert E. Simon a National Planning Pioneer and Reston a National Planning Landmark on September 5.

2003

Thomas J. D'Alesandro IV, Terrabrook vice president and formerly Mobil Land Development Corporation executive vice president, leaves Reston Town Center to become president of The Woodlands in Texas.

Terrabrook sells 12 acres and its partnership interest in One and Two Freedom Square in Reston Town Center, an estimated $305 million disposition in July.

Boston Properties acquires 100 percent ownership of One and Two Freedom Square and the Block 15 commercial office site. KSI Services acquires the Block 16 residential acreage.

Boston Properties leases One Freedom Square office building to Titan Corporation, an electronics firm, and Two Freedom Square to Accenture, an organizational and software management company.

Dulles light-rail debates intensify, with no resolution.

2004

KSI Services, Inc., breaks ground on the 22-story Midtown East and West condominium buildings and Metropolitan Reston apartments, and Midtown Lofts in August.

The Titan Corporation opens its new 280,000-square-foot office in Reston Town Center in the 16-story Two Freedom Square building on September 15.

2005

GRACE moves into its new gallery and offices at Market and St. Francis Street in Reston Town Center.

2006

Robert C. Kettler sponsors the book, *Reston Town Center: A Downtown for the 21st Century*, published by Academy Press.

Midtown's and Metropolitan's residents occupy condos and apartments in the fall.

BIBLIOGRAPHY

ARCHIVES, PLANS, AND DOCUMENTS

Bohl, Charles C. "The Social, Civic and Symbolic Functions of the Public Realm: A Comparative Study of New Urbanist Town Centers and Conventional Shopping Centers." PhD diss., University of North Carolina at Chapel Hill, 2004.

Crane, David A., and Partners. Reston Town Center: Concept Plan and Program, November 1, 1974.

Planned Community Archives, George Mason University, Fairfax, Virginia. www.gmu.edu

Sasaki Associates. "Reston Town Center: Phase II." September 1992.

Reston Land Corporation. "Reston Town Center.kk" Submitted to a Plan Analysis Session of the Urban Land Institute, October 27–29, 1983. Miami, Florida.

Reston Town Center Association
www.restontowncenter.com

PUBLISHED SOURCES ABOUT RESTON TOWN CENTER

Boyd, Kirsten, and Tom Grubisich. "Town Center Moves Forward." *The Connection*, July 17, 1985.

Bredemeier, Kenneth. "Record $205 Million Paid for Office Building." *The Washington Post*, August 11, 2003.

Coulson, Art. "Town Center Designed for 'Urban Pedestrian.'" *The Reston Times*, December 10, 1986.

Dean, Andrea Openheimer. "New Town Downtown." *Architecture*, December 1991.

Dorr, Maude. "The New Town and Major Spaces." *Progressive Architecture* (June 1964): 192–200.

Forgey, Benjamin. "Quicksilver Mercury: A Gleaming Pavilion of Glass and Steel Joins Reston's Fountain Square Statue." *The Washington Post*, July 31, 1993.

Franklin, Ben. "Downtown Look for a 'New Town.'" *The New York Times*, December 21, 1986.

Gezler, Claudia. "Town Center Work Starts." *The Reston Times*, December 10, 1988.

Harrigan, Lucille, and Alexander von Hoffman. "Happy to Grow: Development and Planning in Fairfax County, Virginia." Joint Center for Housing Studies, Harvard University WO4-2 (February 2004).

Hedgpeth, Dana. "Northern Virginia Set for a Rebound; Developers Demonstrate Confidence That the Housing Market Is Improving." *The Washington Post*, May 10, 2004.

Hutson, Nathan. "Reston: A New Town Enters a New Era." Open Space Preservation and Growth Management PRP, April 22, 2003.

Irwin, Neil. "More Firms Warm Up to Reston." *The Washington Post*, October 27, 2003.

Irvin, Woodrow. "Plan for Reston Skate Park Sent Back to Drawing Board." *The Washington Post*, September 4, 2003.

Kurspahic, Mirza. "Living Up to High Expectations: At First There Was Worry Equity Office Properties Would Not Be a Community Partner." *The Connection*, February 17, 2005.

Langdon, Philip. "Reston Town Center, Filling Up, Will Soon Face Redevelopment." *New Urban News* 10, no. 2 (March 2005): 8–9.

L'Etoile, Allan. "Co-Developer Signing Delays Town Center Plans: Center Rezoning Filed by Reston Land." *The Reston Times*, July 18, 1985.

Lemke, Tim. "Reston Project Targets Wealthy." *The Washington Times*, February 20, 2004.

Lerner, Michele. "Forty-year-old Reston Comes into Its Own." *The Washington Times*, July 9, 2004.

Lewis, Pam and Charles Lewis. "Perspective on Reston." *The Reston Times*, Janurary 21, 1987.

Louka, Loukia. "Town Center Plans Approved." *The Reston Times*, February 18, 1987.

McAllister, Marcia. "Reston Land Files Application for Long-Awaited Town Center." *The Wazshingtn Post*, July 20, 1985.

Murdock, James. "Corporations Absorbing NoVA Office Stock; Developers Building on Spec. *Commercial Property News*, March 1, 2004.

Nesmith, Lynn. "News." *Architecture Magazine*, February 1987.

Netherton, Nan. *Reston: New Town in the Old Dominion*. Norfolk, VA: The Donning Company, 1989.

Rensbarger, Fran. "An 'Old' Downtown Now Taking Shape." *New York Times*, November 11, 1990.

"Reston Goes 'Downtown.'" *Metropolitan Home*, September, 1987.

"Reston Retooled: Columbia Take Note." *The Washington Post*, September 21, 2003.

"Reston Town Center," The Urban Land Institute: Project Reference File, July–September 1991.

"RTKL Associates Selected to Design New Town Center for Reston." *Architecture Magazine*, February 1987.

Silverman, Suzanne. "A Word with Kenneth Himmel." *Commercial Property News, CPN Online*, June 6, 2003.

Simmons, Lise Hausrath. *Debate is On: Is Reston Ready to Be a Town, City?* www.timescommunity.com, August 3, 2004.

Smith, Leef. "Statue Didn't Just Walk Away; First Clue Was Man Carrying Off Very Still Woman. *The Washington Post*, May 26, 2004.

———. "The Suburbs Go to Town." *The Washington Post*, January 18, 2004.

"Town Center Parking: Dong it Right from the Start." *The Reston Times*, April 13, 1988.

"Town Center Subsidized Housing Eyed: Plan Draws Kudos, Jeers from Groups." *The Reston Times*, July 8, 1987.

"Traffic Count Snarls Town Center." *The Reston Times*, November 26, 1986.

Watt, Dan, ed. *Reston: The First Twenty Years*. Reston, VA: Reston Publishing Company, 1985.

PUBLISHED SOURCES: URBANISM AND TOWN CENTERS

Adams, Eric. *Architecture* 87, no. 5 (May 1998): 91.

Appleby, Julie. "Good Centers Keep Elderly Active, Safe." *USA Today*, May 25, 2004.

Barnett, Jonathan. "Edge Cities to Real Cities." *Planning*, November 2002.

Bloom, Nicholas Dagen, *Suburban Alchemy: The 1960s New Towns and the Transformation of the American Dream*. Columbus: Ohio State University Press, 2001.

Bohl, Charles C. *Place-Making: Developing Town Centers, Main Streets, and Urban Villages*. Washington, D. C.: Urban Land Institute, 2002.

Diamonstein, Barbara. *American Architecture Now*. II. New York: Rizzoli, 1985, 43–51.

Dorr, Maude. "The New Town & Major Spaces." *Progressive Architecture*, June 1964: 192–200.

The Economist, 307, no. 7546 (April 16, 1988): S8 3.

Hopkins, Lewis D., Robert C. Kettler, George J. Pillorge, Alan L. Ward, and Sam Bass Warner Jr. "Designing New Towns." *Landscape Architecture/LA Forum*, December 1988.

Kotkin, Joel. *The City: A Global History*. New York: Modern Library Chronicles, 2005.

Langdon, Philip. *A Better Place to Live: Reshaping the American Suburb*. Amherst: University of Massachusetts Press, 1994.

———. "A Good Place to Live." *The Atlantic Monthly* 261, no. 3 (March 1988): 39–60.

———. "Pumping Up Suburban Downtowns." *Planning* 56, no. 7 (July 1990): 22–28.

———. "_____." *Governing* 11, no. 9 (June 1998): 24–28.

Lee, Thomas L. "Place Making in Suburbia." *ULI Los Angeles*, November 28, 2000, http://www.uli-la.org/publications/item.php?id=11.

Leinberger, Christopher B. "Financing Progressive Development." *Capital Xchange*. The Brookings Institution, May 2001. Also available online at http://www.brookings.edu.

———. "The Shape of Downtown." *Urban Land* (Nov/Dec 2004): 68–75.

Lockwood, Charles. "Putting the Urb in the Suburbs." *Planning* 63, no. 6 (June 1997): 18–21.

Marshall, Alex."Building New Urbanism: Less Filling, But Not So Tasty." *Builder Magazine*, November 30, 1999.

McMahon, Edward T. "Smart Growth Trends." *Planning Commissioners Journal* 33 (Winter 1999): 4–5.

Olsen, Joshua. "Open Space May Not Be All that It's Cracked Up to Be." *Planning*, September 1999.

Pierce, Neil. "Public is Buying into the Concept of Town Centers with a Variety of Services." *The Plain Dealer*, February 16, 2003.

Postrel, Virginia. *The Substance of Style: How the Rise of Aesthetic Value is Remaking Commerce, Culture, and Consciousness*. New York: HarperCollins Publishers, 2003.

RTKL Associates. "New Generation of Mixed-Use." *Retail Traffic Magazine*, September 1, 2001.

Rybczynski, Witold. "Living Downtown." *Wharton Real Estate Review* IV, no. 1 (Spring 2000): 5–12.

Rykwert, Joseph. *The Idea of a Town: The Anthropology of Urban Form in Rome, Italy, and The Ancient World*. Cambridge: The MIT Press, 1988.

Schwanke, Dean, et al. *Mixed-Use Development Handbook*. Washington, D. C.: Urban Land Institute, 2003.

Scully, Vincent. "The American City in A.D. 2025: A Considered Opinion." *The Brookings Review* 18, no. 3 (Summer 2000): 2–3.

Smart Growth Network. *Getting to Smart Growth II: 100 More Policies for Implementation*. Washington, DC: International City/County Management Association, 2004. Also available online at http://www.icma.org.

Steuteville, Robert. "Developer Fascination with Urban Center Grows." *New Urban News*, October/November 2003.

Urban Land Institute. "The Future of Town Centers and Main Streets." Fifth Annual Place Making Conference. Reston Town Center, Virginia, September 11–13, 2003.

Walk, Jesse. "Radical 'burbs." *Reason* 34, no. 8 (January 2003): 50–55.

ENDNOTES

INTRODUCTION: A DOWNTOWN FOR THE 21ST CENTURY/BOHL

1. The Fountain Square office buildings were fully leased by year-end 1992.

2. Kenneth Bredemeier, "Record $205 Million Paid for Office Buildings," *The Washington Post* (August 11, 2003): E01.

3. Rob Steuteville, "Urban Core Cuts Traffic in Reston by Nearly Half," *New Urban News* 5, no. 6 (October/November 2000): 16.

4. Mirza Kurspahic "Losing Affordable Housing: Area's Economic Growth Causes Higher Housing Costs and Less Available Affordable Units," *The Connection Newspapers* (March 3, 2005) http://www.connectionnewspapers.com/printarticle.asp?article=47179.

5. Charles C. Bohl, "The Social, Civic and Symbolic Functions of the Public Realm: A Comparative Study of New Urbanist Town Centers and Conventional Shopping Centers" (PhD diss., University of North Carolina at Chapel Hill, 2004)

CERTAINTY TO FLEXIBILITY: PLANNING AND DESIGN HISTORY, 1963–2005 / WARD

1. William Whittlesey retired from the firm before major work on the new town got underway.

2. David A. Crane and Partners, "Reston Town Center: Concept Plan and Program," November 1974.

3. Summarized by Hunter Richardson of Reston Land Corporation from taped recordings of the ULI sessions, Fall 1983.

4. The Hyatt Regency Reston Hotel was built with 511 rooms.

5. *Commercial Property News*, June 16, 2003.

6. Witold Rybczynski, "Living Downtown." *Wharton Real Estate Review* IV, no. 1 (Spring 2000): 5–12.

7. Christopher Leinberger, "The Shape of Downtown." *Urban Land* (Nov/Dec 2004): 68–75.

BUILDING AN URBAN NEIGHBORHOOD / KETTLER

1. Joint Center for Housing Studies of Harvard University, *The State of the Nation's Housing 2004* [on-line]; available from http://www.jchs.harvard.edu/publications/markets/son2004.pdf; Internet; accessed 11 June 2005.

2. MSN Money, *Number of $1 million dollar homes has doubled* [on-line]; available from http://moneycentral.msn.com/content/invest/extra/P119226.asp?; Internet; accessed 25 May 2005.

3. KSI is the largest developer and manager of affordable housing in the Washington, D.C. metropolitan area. Reston Town Center, however, was not viewed as an appropriate affordable-housing location, rather one that was prime for market-rate and high-end housing.

4. Ray Smith, *Property Firms Pitch "Rondo" Units Again* [on-line]; available from http://www.realestatejournal.com/propertyreport/residential/20040112-smith.html; Internet; accessed 9 June 2005.

5. Clay Risen, *McMansion Meets Soho* [on-line]; available from http://slate.msn.com/id/2113614; Internet; accessed 2 March 2005.

RESTON TOWN CENTER BUILDINGS

FOUNTAIN SQUARE I AND II, 1990
530,000 s. f. office
200,000 s. f. retail and restaurants
11-screen movie theater
3 to 10 stories
Reston Land Corporation and
    Himmel/MKDG, developers
RTKL Associates, architect
Sasaki Associates, landscape architect

HYATT REGENCY RESTON HOTEL,
    1990–91
511 rooms
14 stories
Reston Land Corporation and
    Himmel/MKDG, developers
RTKL Associates, architect

WEST MARKET, 1998 AND 2000
322-unit condominium and townhouses
3 stories
Miller & Smith, developer
George Papageorge, architect

STRATFORD HOUSE AND STRATFORD
    PARK, 2000–2001
342-unit condominium
14 stories and 4 stories
Albert Small, Sr., developer
Torti Gallas and Partners, architect

ONE FREEDOM SQUARE, 2000
400,000 s. f. office
16,000 s. f. retail
18 stories
Terrabrook/Boston Properties,
    developers
The Smith Group, architect
Sasaki Associates, landscape architect

TWO FREEDOM SQUARE, 2002
400,000 s. f. office
24,000 s. f. retail
16 stories
Terrabrook/Boston Properties,
    developer
The Smith Group, architect
Sasaki Associates, landscape architect

THE SAVOY, 2003–2004
365-unit condominium
4 stories
Trammell Crow Residential, developer
Crescent Heights, condominium
    developer
Lessard Group Architects, architect

MARKET STREET AT TOWN CENTER,
    2003
333-unit condominium
4 stories
Trammell Crow Residential, developer
Lessard Group Architects, architect

THE PARAMOUNT, 2004
298-unit condominium
14 stories
Diamond Properties, developer
S K & I, architect

SALLIE MAE HEADQUARTERS, 2005
240,000 s. f. office and conference
8 stories
Boston Properties and J. Studley,
    project management
Boggs and Partners Architects, architect

RESTON TOWN SQUARE, 2005
1.25 acres
KSI Services, Inc., developer
Sasaki Associates, landscape architect

MIDTOWN EAST AND WEST, 2006
293-unit condominium
21 stories
16,000 s. f. retail
KSI Services, Inc., developer
Lessard Group Architects, architect

MIDTOWN LOFTS, 2006
78-unit condominium
5 to 7 stories
KSI Services, Inc., developer
CMSS Architects, architects

METROPOLITAN AT RESTON TOWN
    CENTER, 2006
288-unit apartment
KSI Services, Inc., developer
Lessard Group Architects, architect

BLOCK 16, FUTURE
341-unit condominium
34,000 square retail
15 stories
KSI Services, Inc., developer
Robert A. M. Stern Associates, architect

BLOCK 14 AND 15, FUTURE
580,000 s. f. office
60,000 s. f. retail
10 stories
Boston Properties, developer
The Smith Group, architect

ACKNOWLEDGMENTS

THIS BOOK COULD NOT have been done without Robert C. Kettler, chairman of KSI Services, who initiated and supported the collaboration to produce this book. It was his intent to document the interesting and complex story behind the making of this new and distinctly urban place in the suburbs.

When Bob Kettler first discussed his idea for the book, I suggested we trust Jan Cigliano, publisher of Academy Press—which consistently produces beautiful books on the built environment—to publish this volume on Reston Town Center. Jan is a writer and authority on new towns, and has been a master at pulling together the pieces of this book in a timely way. Jan has helped to coalesce in one coherent volume the work of respected journalists Tom Vanderbilt and Philip Langdon, new-town expert Charles C. Bohl, and architect Robert. A. M. Stern; chapters by two of the town center's developers, Thomas D'Alesandro and Robert Kettler; and my own history of the planning and design of the town center.

Thanks to Sara E. Stemen, graphic designer, who artfully combined the text, archival plans, older photographs, with striking new photographs by Bryan Becker and perspective aerial maps by Jane Sheinman. Laura London and Sarah Davidson of KSI helped coordinate the company's significant contributions to the book, with research assistance by Kevin Peterkin. Stephanie Duck scoured archives and libraries to collate primary and published reference material used by each of the contributors. Veronica Fletcher of the Planned Community Archives at George Mason University helped identify and reproduce some original plans of Reston Town Center.

Many individuals graciously provided personal perspectives, recollections, and insights. Judy Buckley, the sales manager at KSI's Midtown condominiums, offered insight on the residential market to Philip Langdon and the book's publicist, Liz Wainger of Wainger Communications. John Assadorian, Seth Harry, Laurence Aurback, and Peter Otteni and Ray Ritchey of Boston Properties graciously provided information and assistance to the publication.

I am particularly grateful to architect and planner William Conklin who helped me understand the fascinating story of the early years at Reston under Robert E. Simon's leadership. James Todd provided an excellent summary during his leadership of both the Gulf Reston and early Mobil Reston periods. Architect and urban designer George Pillorgé dug deep into his files and memories to resurrect his initial thinking and schemes that are the basis for the town center which opened in 1990. As I put together my chapter based on the input from these individuals, along with my own 20-year involvement at Reston, I tested and refined my ideas in discussions with Carol Pullekines. Carol, who is also my wife, is a superb writer who challenged my thinking and helped bring clarity to my ideas through her editing.

And finally, I am grateful to Robert E. Simon, who shared his recollections of the visionary thoughts for the town center in the early years of Reston. I hope we have at least partially realized his aspirations for the center of Reston.

Alan Ward
Watertown, Massachusetts

CONTRIBUTORS

ALAN WARD, editor and author of "Certainty to Flexibility: Planning and Design History" and "Toward an Organic Model for Cities," is a principal at Sasaki Associates, a planning and design firm based in Watertown, Massachusetts. He has worked as a landscape architect and urban designer on Reston Town Center for almost 20 years; as well as other landmark projects, including the Dallas Arts District, Cleveland Gateway Sports District, The Woodlands Town Center, and the Master Plan for the 2008 Beijing Olympic Games. With a degree in architecture from University of Cincinnati and landscape architecture from Harvard University, Mr. Ward has taught in both fields, and is author and photographer of *American Designed Landscapes: A Photographic Interpretation* (2003). He was a visiting artist at the American Academy in Rome in 2002.

CHARLES C. BOHL, author of the "Introduction: A Downtown for the 21st Century," wrote *Place Making: Town Center, Main Streets and Transit Villages* (2002), a best-selling book published by the Urban Land Institute and regarded as the seminal work on the subject of place making. Mr. Bohl is director of the Knight Program in Community Building at the University of Miami and teaches planning, design, and development of livable communities in the school of architecture. The Knight Program trains mid-career community leaders, real estate professionals, policymakers, and designers. He has contributed scholarly essays to *The Ecological Alternative to Sub-urbanization* and *This House is Home: Interdisciplinary Perspectives on Affordable Homeownership*, and has written for *Wharton Real Estate Review*, *Journal of Markets and Morality*, and *Housing Policy Debate*. Mr. Bohl's introduction to *Reston Town Center* will appraise the evolving town center in the context of national peers and precedents.

RACHEL S. COX, contributing writer of "Developing Reston Town Center," is a freelance writer based in Washington, D.C. She writes frequently about design, planning, and environmental issues, notably for *CQ Researcher*, and also for *The Washington Post*, *Preservation*, *Landscape Architecture*, and *Garden Design*, among others. She wrote about exemplary land development for the book *Hollin Hills: Community of Vision*. She was an editor at *Historic Preservation* magazine and a staff writer at *Time-Life Books*. Her experience in the planning realm includes work at the Bureau of Land Management and the Massachusetts Office of Coastal Zone Management. She is a cum laude graduate of Harvard College and studied architectural history at UCLA.

THOMAS J. D'ALESANDRO IV, author of "Developing Reston Town Center," is a senior vice president for General Growth, Inc. As an executive and civic leader for over twenty years, he has guided the development of several residential, commercial, recreational, and civic real estate projects. He previously served as president of The Woodlands Operating Company during 2003–2005, where he oversaw development of The Woodlands, a 27,000-acre master-planned community north of Houston, Texas; and for several years led development of Reston Town Center for Mobil Land Development Corporation. During this time, Reston was named a national planning landmark by the American Planning Association, and the town center received the American Institute of Architects' urban design award of excellence in 1991. Mr. D'Alesandro holds a master's from the Darden School of Business at the University of Virginia, a master of arts from the University of Chicago, and a bachelor of arts from Loyola College in Baltimore, Maryland.

ROBERT C. KETTLER, the book's sponsor and author of "Building an Urban Neighborhood," is chairman and founder of KSI Services, Inc. A third-generation builder, he began his career in 1973 renovating residential and commercial real estate and building new home communities in Washington, D.C. In 1982 he began developing planned communities in Northern Virginia. At Reston Town Center, KSI is developing 1,000 residential units at its Midtown community. KSI Services has received hundreds of awards for housing design, land planning, and urban design. It is the largest land developer in metropolitan Washington, employing 450 professionals, with a diverse development portfolio of residential and commercial properties, public parks and schools, championship golf courses, and extensive transportation improvements. KSI is ranked among the nation's top fifteen multifamily developers, owning 10,000 apartments in the Washington area, including luxury high-rise apartments and affordable housing. The National Association of Home Builders named Mr. Kettler developer of the year in 1986. He has served on the boards of directors of the Northern Virginia Building Industry Association, Venture America (a venture capital fund), the Washington Metropolitan Area Boys Club, the Potomac School in McLean, Virginia, and St. Patrick's Episcopal School in Washington, D.C. He has served on advisory boards at George Mason University and Northern Virginia Community College. A native Washingtonian, Mr. Kettler attended the George Washington University and American University, where he concentrated in economics and real estate. He and his wife, Charlotte, have four children.

PHILIP LANGDON, *Urban Tastes and Suburban Living*, is senior editor of *New Urban News*, and previously for *Progressive Architecture*. He is author of several books, including *A Better Place to Live: Reshaping the American Suburb* (1994); *Orange Roofs, Golden Arches: The Architecture of American Chain Restaurants* (1986); and *American Houses* (1987). For over twenty years, Mr. Langdon has been writing about design and planning for such magazines as *Urban Land*; *Landscape Architecture*; *Planning*; *Preservation*; *Governing*; and *Architectural Record*. His 1988 *Atlantic Monthly* cover story, "A Good Place to Live," introduced the idea of neotraditional development, more recently known as New Urbanism. He holds a master's in history from Utah State University, and was 2001 Knight Fellow at the University of Miami.

LAURA LEWIS, who contributed to Robert C. Kettler's "Building an Urban Neighborhood," is a freelance writer in Washington, D.C. She began her career writing for National Geographic. She has degrees from Virginia Tech and Georgetown University.

ROBERT E. SIMON, JR., was born in New York City in 1914. After graduating from Harvard University, Simon took over the family real estate management and development business. In 1961, with the proceeds from the sale of a family property, Carnegie Hall, Simon purchased 6,750 acres of land in Fairfax County, Virginia, which would become Reston, Virginia. Reston is now recognized as the foremost planned community in the United States. The planned community, or new town, of Reston emphasized the quality of life for the individual and provide a community where people could live, work, and play. Mr. Simon established the Robert E. Simon Collection as part of the Planned Community Archives at George Mason University, a nonprofit corporation dedicated to improving the quality of community development in the United States through the use of its archival, research, publishing and instructional resources.

RAYMOND A. RITCHEY is executive vice president and head of the Washington, D.C. office of Boston Properties. He is also the national partner-in-charge of acquisitions and business development. Since joining Boston Properties in 1980, Mr. Ritchey has been involved with the Washington office in acquiring, developing, and leasing over 16 million square feet of office, retail, industrial, hotel, and residential development. Mr. Ritchey has leased over 10 million square feet of office and industrial space to institutional, corporate, and government agencies, including the Office of the Comptroller of the Currency; Overseas Private Investment Corporation; NASA; the U.S. International Trade Commission; Shaw Pittman Potts and Trowbridge; the Thurgood Marshall Federal Judiciary Building; TRW; Accenture; and Jones Day Reavis and Pogue. Mr. Ritchey is a graduate of the U.S. Naval Academy in Annapolis, Maryland, and the U. S. Naval Post Graduate School in Monterey, California.

ROBERT A. M. STERN, architect, teacher, and writer, is dean
of the Yale School of Architecture and founder of Robert A.M.
Stern Architects of New York. Mr. Stern's thirty-five-year
career has been dedicated to the idea that architecture and planning must engage in a conversation across time, connecting the
present and future with the past. His longstanding interest in
planning led him to write, with co-author John Massengale,
The Anglo-American Suburb (1981), and he has gone on to collaborate on two of the most important planning projects of our
time: the new town of Celebration, Florida, and the redevelopment of the theater block of New York's 42nd Street. In 1986
Mr. Stern hosted *Pride of Place: Building the American Dream,*
an eight-part, eight-hour documentary television series aired
on the Public Broadcasting System.

TOM VANDERBILT, author of "A Brooklyn Boy in Reston
Town Center: There Should be More Places Like This," is a
New York City-based writer on architecture, design, technol-
ogy, science and other topics. He is contributing editor to *I.D.*
(*International Design*) and *Print Magazine,* and writes regularly
for a range of publications, including: *The New York Times,*
Wired, The Financial Times, Smithsonian, GQ, Preservation,
Slate, Metropolis, Harvard Design Magazine, AIGA Journal,
Cabinet, Artforum, and others. He is author of the book *Survival*
City: Adventures Among the Ruins of Atomic America (Princeton
Architectural Press) and *The Sneaker Book: Anatomy of an*
Industry and Icon. Mr. Vanderbilt has contributed to a number of
books, including *Supercade: A Visual History of the Videogame*
Age and *Comodify Your Dissent: Salvos from the Baffler.* Recent
pieces have ranged from architectural history of the Quonset
hut to the neuroscientific underpinnings of urban navigation.
He graduated in 1991 from the University of Wisconsin, with
honors in history and political science.

BRYAN BECKER, photographer, is a graduate of the Corcoran
School of Art with a Bachelor of Fine Art in Photography. He
is currently advancing his practice of architectural photography
in the Washington, D.C. area. Bryan's photographs capture the
complex interactions and activities that animate our cityscapes.
His photographs have been published in the *Washingtonian,* the
Washington Post, and in *American Libraries,* the magazine of the
American Library Association.

PHOTO CREDITS
For images other than those by Bryan Becker.
page 8 *top*, 20, 26 *left*, 93: Charles C. Bohl; page 10, 184: Jane
Sheinman; page 30, 62 *bottom*: Max MacKenzie; page 36, 60, 63,
64, 65, 89, 108, 109 *left*: Alan Ward; page 37, 39 *bottom*: Planned
Community Archive, George Mason University; page 38–39:
PA/Progressive Architecture, 1964; page 43, 47, 50–54, 69, 178,
183: RTKL Associates; page 56, 58, 62 *top*, 66, 67, 180: Sasaki
Associates; page 118 *right*, 187: Jan Cigliano: page 119–20: Bob
Narod; 124–37, 182: Robert A. McComus; page 172, 174, 177:
Robert A. M. Stern Architects.

INDEX

Accenture (Andersen Consulting), 15, 99–100
affordable housing. *See under* housing
Almere, The Netherlands, 165
American Institute of Architects (AIA), 66
Andersen Consulting. *See* Accenture (Andersen Consulting)
apartments, 102
architects, 85
architectural competition
    entries, *50–54*
    phase I design, 49–55
architectural continuity guidelines, 70
architectural identity, 19, 70, 128
architectural style
    art deco, 95
    classicism, 55
    modernism, 9–10, 36
art deco style, 95
art gallery, design of, 91
awards, design, 66

Balwin Park, 20
Barnes & Noble, 92
BDM International, 100
Bensman, Joseph, 141
Berube, Alan, 154
Best Buy, 92
block pattern. *See* grid street pattern
Bloomsbury District, London, 40
Boca Raton, Florida, 20, 24
Bohl, Charles C., 2, 5–21, 201
Boston Properties, 13–14, 69, 97, 99, 104, 151
Brookings Institution, 154
Brooks, David, 165
Bryant Park, New York City, 168
building design details, 187
business improvement districts, 149–151

Calabrese, Antonio, 83
cars and pedestrians, interaction of, 59–61
Celebration, Florida, 25, 143–145
Cemin, Saint Clair, 61
Chace, Arnold B., 143
Childs, David, 49
churches, 24
cities
    evolution of, 129, 135, 164, 168, 181

city blocks. *See* grid street pattern
City Center, Denver, 49
City Place, West Palm Beach, FL, 21
city centers. *See* downtowns; town centers
city-making. *See* place-making
city planning. *See* urban planning
civic events and institutions, 23–25, 133
classicism (architecture), 55
Cleveland, James (Jim), 1, 49, 78, 81
collaboration, design, 85–87
commercial space, 73
commercial success, 109–110
community, sense of, 128, 129, 136
community planning movement, 142
comprehensive development plan, 78, 79
concerts, 92
condominiums, 93–94, 101, *118*
Congress for the New Urbanism, 85
Conklin, William, 9, 35, 40, 181
Cooley Godward, 100
corporate headquarters, 99–100, 113
Cox, Rachel S., 105, 201
Crane, David A., 41–43, *42*, 44
"creative class," growth of, 113–114
cultural center, 91–92

D'Alesandro, Thomas J., 1, 3, 13, 19, 23, 66, 67, 70,
    75, 105
    "Developing Reston Town Center," 75–105
David A. Crane and Partners, 41–43, *42*
Davis, Marvin, 90
density, urban, 1, 92, 128, 132
design, building, 187
design awards, 66
design continuity guidelines, 70
design details, importance of, 187
design framework, flexible, 183
developers, financial resources of, 184
development partnerships, 49, 81–82, 85–87, 97,
    102, 120
development process, 181
    of last remaining parcels, 102–105
    phase I, 85
    phase II, 95–101
Discovery Square, *98*
Disney, Walt, 163
downtowns, 8–9, 71–73, 77, 128, 130, 132. *See also*

    town centers
    critical population mass for, 14, 71–72
    established, 72–73
    and free speech rights, 71, 151
    public character of, 149
Dulles corridor, 101–102
Dulles International Airport, 79
    access to, 145
Dulles Toll Road, 34
    opening of, 79
    proposed bridge over, 43

edge cities, 148–149, 167
Edge City, 148
Elkjer, William, 81, 93
enclosed shopping environments, 41–43
Equity Office Properties, 97, 104, 150–151
events and festivals, 59–61, 91–92, 154
exurban landscape (U.S.)
    flight from, 164–167

Fairfax County, Virginia, 19, 83
    Board of Supervisors, 35, 82–83
    eight-mile zoning restriction, 87
    income demographics, 113
    zoning policies, 18
festivals. *See* events and festivals
Florance, Colden (Coke), 95
Florida, Richard, 113
Forgey, Benjamin, 61
Fountain Square, *6*, 15, *16*, 59–61, *63*, *169*
    Christmas tree, 161
    design for (1986), 54
    and sense of place, 160
Fountain Square plaza, 23, *24*, 80, *144*, 159–160
    cultural center designs for, 91–92
    flexible design for, 55
    outdoor events in, 59–61
Freedom Square, *19*, 69–70, *115*
    office towers, 69–70
    parking garage, *65*
    plaza, *70*
Frey, William H., 154
future redevelopment, 181

gallery building, design of, 91
garden city model, 33

Garreau, Joel, 148
George, Phil, 85
George Mason University, 113
Georgetown (Washington, DC), 111, 119
Gladstone, Robert, 41, 48, 134
government agencies and contractors, 113
GRACE gallery, 23–25
Graham, Vince, 15
green spaces, 34, 63–65, 67–69
Greenbelt towns, 34
greenbelts, 33–34
greenspace. See green spaces
grid street pattern, 42, 44–45, 48, 66–67, 151
    flexibility of, 181
    plan for (1983), 44
ground-floor retail. See shopping district
Grubisch, Tom, 55
Gulf Oil Corporation, 41, 44, 78
Gulf Reston. See Gulf Oil Corporation

Hagelis, Al, 93
Hardy Holzman Pfeiffer, 91
Harland Bartholomew and Associates, 35
Harry, Seth, 149
Harvard University, "New Communities Project,"
    44
Henderer, Rod, 85
Hendrix, William, 69
Henry, Peter, 94
Heron House, 95
high-density, mixed use development, 145, 184, 184.
    See also under mixed-use
high-rise buildings, 66–67, 71, 95, 101, 115–117, 145
    Freedom Square office towers, 69
    Midtown condominiums, 119
high-technology firms, 101
Himmel, Kenneth (Ken), 49, 50, 56, 58, 59, 65, 82,
    85–87
Himmel/MKDG, 49, 49, 85, 90
historic cities, evolution of, 135
homebuilders, 94
hospitality industry. See hotels
hotels, 19, 86, 104
housing, 14, 19–21. See also residential develop-
    ments
    affordable, 19–20
    apartments, 102
    comparative cost of, 115
    condominiums, 93–94, 101, 118
    importance of in mixed-use development, 92–93
    scarcity of, 114
Howard, Ebenezer, 33
HUD. See U.S. Dept. of Housing and Urban
    Development (HUD)
Hyatt Regency Hotel, 19, 86, 152

ice rink, 15, 91–92, 103, 158, 159, 160, 161
infrastructure, commercial, 73
institutions, 23–24, 132–33

International Council of Shopping Centers, 87

Jacobs, Jane, 153

Kaylor, Jim, 14
Kentlands, MD, 25
Kettler, Robert C., iv, 1–3, 13, 14, 104, 125, 126,
    128–131, 133–137, 199, 202.
    "Building an Urban Neighborhood," 107–21.
Keyes Condon Florance (KCF), 95, 99
Kohn Pederson Fox, 49, 51
Koolhaas, Rem, 165
Krier, Leon, 153
Krocker, Michelle, 20
KSI Services, iv, 14, 71, 104, 111, 117, 118, 119

labor force, growth of, 111–113
    "creative class" within, 113–114
Lake Anne Plaza, 163
Lake Anne Village Center, 8, 9–11, 35–36, 36
design recognition of, 36
road link to, 41
land use policies. See zoning policies
landscape and building plan, 66
landscape plan (1988–1990), 56–66
landscape reconnaissance plan, 56
landscape studies, 57, 58
Langdon, Philip, 3, 15, 19, 202
    "Urban Tastes and Suburban Living," 138–55.
Latham Watkins, 100
leasing
    commercial, 87, 109–110
    corporate, 100
    office, 90
Leinberger, Christopher, 73
Lerner, Ted, 79
Lerner Enterprises, 94
Lessard, Chris, 102, 104
Lessard Group Architects, 1, 102, 104
Lewis, Laura, 121, 202
Library Street, sidewalk dining, 72
light rail transit, 131
live-work-play environments, 133
low-density development
    outside urban core, 150
Lucas, Frank, 85

map
    aerial, 184
    axonometric, 13
Market Street, 9, 17, 30, 43, 59–61
    cars and pedestrians on, 59
    as organizing element, 46
    as shopping district, 59
    sidewalk landscaping of, 110, 124, 145
    streetscape design, 85
    view looking west, 86
Mashpee Commons, Massachusetts, 20, 25, 143
mass transit, 162

light rail, 135
master plan
    choice of site for, 37–40, 41, 183
    long-term commitment to, 184
master-planned communities, 32, 105
Mayer, Albert, 35
Mendenhall, Randa, 91
merchants, retail. See retail merchants
Mercury (sculpture and fountain), 15, 24, 55, 62, 161
    as central landmark, 61
Metrorail station (proposed), 43, 131
Miami Lakes Town Center, 20
Midtown, 115, 118, 119, 167
    selling prices of, 119
neighborhood, 14, 104, 116, 117
    as final step in Reston Town Center, 120
    luxury amenities of, 119
    resident incomes in, 120
Miller, Linda, 91
Miller & Smith, 94
Milton Keynes (planned community), England, 165
mixed-use
    design, 120, 121
    environment, 56–59, 81, 84, 85, 109, 132, 135,
        154–155
mixed-use development, 132, 142
    economic pressures against, 90
    importance of housing in, 92
Mizner Park, FL, 20, 24, 25
Mobil Oil Corporation, 41, 44, 79, 97. See also
    Reston Land Corporation (RLC)
Mobil Reston. See Mobil Oil Corporation
moderate-income housing. See under housing
modernism (architecture), 9–10, 36
Modjeska, Gary, 104
Moore, Charles, 163
movie theater, 166, 167
Multiplex cinema, 166, 167
museums. See gallery building, design of

neighborhoods, 111, 117
    24-hour, 71–72
new cities. See new towns
"New Communities Project," 44
new town centers, 33. See also new urbanism; town
    centers
    free speech rights in, 151
new towns, 142, 164–165
    garden city model, 33
new urbanism, 18, 143, 163. See also town centers;
    urbanism
New York Times, 164
northern Virginia. See also Washington, D.C.-area
    commercial real estate market in, 99
    real estate market of, 13

Oak Park Condominium, 93–94
occupancy rates. See also leasing office, 90
office buildings, 87, 97–101, 100, 112

at Fountain Square, 61
Office for Metropolitain Architecture, 165
office occupancy rates, 90
office space, 128
office towers, 69–70
office workers, *112*
On Paradise Drive, 165
One Fountain Square
    north entrance, *60*
One Freedom Square, *19*, 69, *86*, 95, *96*, *99*
    corporate tenant for, 99–100
    retail shops in, *17*
open spaces, 95–96, 186
Oracle Corporation, 100
Orenco Station Town Center, 20
Orlando, FL, 20
outdoor events, 59–61, 92
outdoor plaza dining, *140*
ownership, changes in, 41, 44, 78–79, 90, 97,
    104–105

Papageorge, George, 94
Paramount, The, 14
parking
    garages, 18, *22*, *65*
    shared, 65
parks, 63–64, 67–69, 95
partnerships, development. *See* development part-
    nerships
pavilion, Fountain Square, *16*, 23, 91–92
pedestrian barriers, 152
pedestrian bridge, *147*
pedestrian mall (proposed), 41–43
pedestrian-oriented communities, 111, 143, 154–155
pedestrians and cars, interaction of, 59–61
Pennino, Martha, 83
Peterson Companies, 93
Pillorgè, George, 44
place, sense of, 19, 25, 142, 160
place-making, 9, 19, 134, 142, 164
    experiment in, 155
place markers, *161*
planning. *See* urban planning
plans, proposed. *See also* schemes, proposed
    David A. Crane & Partners (1974), 41–43, *42*
    Whittlesey & Conklin (1963), *185*
plazas
    Fountain Square, *24*, *26*, 59–61, 91–92, *146*
    Freedom Square, *70*
    storefronts opening onto, *147*
population density, 71–73
Portland, OR, 20
Portofino, Italy, 36
Pritchard, Edgar, 83
Progressive Architecture (PA), 40
property values, 18, 110, 126, 128, 131, 137.
proposals (plans). *See* plans, proposed; schemes,
    proposed

public places, 25, 186
    legal aspects of, 71, 149, 151
public transportation. *See* mass transit

Radburn, New Jersey, 33, 35
real estate, commercial, 87–88, 89–90
real estate, residential. *See* housing; residential
    developments
real estate development. *See also* development
    process
    suburban vs. urban, 7–8
redevelopment, future, 181
rental units. *See* apartments
residential base (population), 70–71, 126
residential developments, 111. *See also* housing
    Heron House, 95
    Midtown neighborhood, 117
    proposed, 71
    regional limitations of, 114
    Stratford House, 101
    in West Market neighborhood, 93–94
residential district, 66–69
Reston, Virginia
    commercial space in, 73
    general plan (1988), *32*
    master plan (1963), *37*
    as "new town," *142*
    origin of name, 34
    population growth of, 48–49
    proximity to Dulles Airport, 80–81
    suburban development in, 152
    village centers of, 142–143
Reston Community Association (RCA), 78
Reston Land Corporation (RLC), 44, 49, 67, 81, 90,
    95. *See also* Mobil Oil Corporation
Reston Overlook, *98*
Reston Park, *19*, 63–65, *64*, *118*, *186*
Reston Parkway, *22*, 27, 37, 83
    connection to Market Street, 46
Reston Town Center
    axonometric map of, 13, 184
    civic uses of, 23–25 (See also civic events and
        institutions)
    "corporate" ambience of, 153
    as desirable corporate address, 99–101
    early economic success of, 11–13
    future evolution of, 73
    initial criticism of, 109
    ownership and control of, 41, 78–79 (See also
        ownership, changes in)
    periphery of, 159–160
    phase II extension, 66–73, 97–101
    phase II postponement, 90
    plan revisions (1994), *69*
    planning studies (1989), *66*
    population density of, 71
    premium value of, 126, 128, 131, 137, 155
    private ownership of streets in, 149

    property values in, 18, 110
    proposed development plans (1974), *42*
    proposed schemes of (1963), *38–39*
    as prototype new city, 164
    as residential neighborhood, 101–102
    RTKL plans for (1983–1986), 44–46
    as shopping center, 87
    site plan modification (1984–1986), *47*
    site plan variations, *44*, *45*
    siting of, 37
    strategic positioning of, 41
    urban character of, *142*
    visions for, 124–137
Reston Town Center Pavilion, *16*, *102*
Reston Town Square, 67–69, *68*, 95
retail
    boutiques, *110*
    competition, 87
    development, 79
    infrastructure, 71–72
retail destinations
    critical mass and mix of, 94, 125
retail merchants, 87–89
    eight-mile zoning restriction on, 87
    national chain, 92–93
    sales-per-foot of, 110
Richardson, J. Hunter, 47, 81
Ritchey, Joseph, 90, 100
Ritchey, Raymond A. (Ray), 3, 97, *124–135*, *137*,
    202
roads and parkways, 22
    construction of, 83
    as pedestrian barriers, 152
Rossant, James, 35
Rouse, James, 87
RTKL Associates, 1, 11, 22, *44*, 44–48, 49–55, *53*,
    60, *62*, 66, 81, 82, 85, 92, 95, 164
    master plan (1990) with Sasaki Associates, *185*
    phase I plan, 55
Rybczynski, Witold, 71–72

Sasaki Associates, 1, 22, *56*, 56–59, *57*, *58*, *62*, 63,
    66, *67–69*, 85
    design of Reston Town Square, 95
    master plan (1990) with RTKL, *185*
Savoy, The, *116*, 152, 153
schemes, proposed, *38–39*, 40. *See also* plans, pro-
    posed
Scogin, Mark, 91
Scogin Elam & Bray, 91
sense of place, 19, 25, 160
shared parking, 65
shopping centers, 87, 136
shopping district, 71–72, *84*. *See also under* retail
    design of, 85
    shops and restaurants in, *84*, *86*
SI International, 149
sidewalk dining, *72*

sidewalks, 59
Simon, Robert E., 1, 3, 9, 33, 34, 40, 48, 77–78, 79,
    83, 94, *124–130, 132–137*, 142, 163, 164,
    181, *182*, 202
    "Visions for the Town Center: A Dialogue," 9,
        124–137
site plan (Reston Town Center)
    modification (1984–1986), *47*
    RLC and RTKL(1983), *44*
    RTKL(1986), *54*
skating rink. *See* ice rink
Skidmore Owings & Merrill (SOM), 49–55
skyline, 68–70, 145
"skyscrapers." *See* high-rise buildings
Small, Albert, Sr., 101
Small Town in Mass Society, 141
smart growth, 18
Smith, Cloethiel Woodward, 35, 36
Smith Group, 1, 69, 99
Somerset House Condominium Towers (Chevy
    Chase, Maryland), 101
Southern Engineering, 101
Southlake, Texas, 24
Spectrum, The, 94
sprawl, 1, 32, 136, 167
Stein, Clarence, 33
Stern, Robert A.M., 1, 3, 170–77, 203
storefront design, *84*, 85, *86*, *187*
Storrs, Douglas, 143
Stratford House, 101, *116*
street grid. *See* grid street pattern
street signage, *146*
streetfront design, 59
streets
    private ownership of, 71, 149, 151
    social aspects of, *160*, 160–162
streetscapes, allure of, 151
structured parking. *See* parking
suburban development, 32–33. *See also* real estate
    development
    future town centers for, 26
    limitations on, 114
    urban core amid, 126, 130
suburban sprawl. *See* sprawl
suburbia
    changing demography of, 154
    contrast with urban landscape, 160

Terrabrook, 97, 99–100, 102, 117
    divestment of holdings by, 104
The Woodlands (Texas), 105

theater, movie, *166*, 167
Thompson Ventulett Stainback, 49, *52*
Tiersch, Wolf, 91, 93
Titan Corporation, 100
Todd, James, 41, 44, 46–47, 94
Torti, John, 101
towers. *See* high-rise buildings
town centers, 124–127, 143. *See also* downtowns;
    urban planning
    civic institutions in, 24–25
    demand for housing in, 20–21
    flexible zoning for, 67
    planning and design of, 9–11
    population requirement of, 164
    Reston as model for, 25–26
    romantic visions of, 163
    traditional concept of, 141
town-making. *See* place-making
town planning. *See also* town centers; urban plan-
    ning
    masterplan approach to, 35
traffic congestion, 83
    in edge cities, 148–149
traffic engineering standards, 152–153
Trammell Crow Residential (TCR), 14, 102, 152
transit station, 41. *See also* mass transit
trees, street, 63
Two Freedom Square, *19*, 69, *99*
Tysons Corner, 83, 99, 100, 148–149, 167
Tysons Corner Center, 79
Tysons Corner Mall, 87

ULI. *See* Urban Land Institute (ULI)
urban core (Reston Town Center), 109
    geographic center of, 103–104
    high-density environment of, 151
    phase one site plan for, *57*
    population density of, 71
    westward extension of, *57*
urban design awards, 66
urban design plan
    modifications for Reston Town Center, 37–47
    street grid as organizing principle in, 48, 151
Urban Land, 73
Urban Land Institute (ULI), 41, 47, 81
urban planning, 11–13, 127–137, 163–164. *See also*
    town centers
    modernism in, 9–10
    political aspects of, 131
    process of, 136, 181–187
urban sprawl. *See* sprawl

urbanism, 7, 9, 18, 159, 167–168. *See also* new
    urbanism
    classic, 167
    the ideal city environment, 153–154
    inside-out, 164
    traditional, 11
U.S. Dept. of Housing and Urban Development
    (HUD), 44

Vanderbilt, Tom, 3, 7, 15, 203
"vertical planned community," 117
Vidich, Arthur J., 141
village centers, 35–36
Virginia Department of Transportation (VDOT)
    traffic engineering standards of, 152–153
vision (big picture), 32–35, *77–78*, 182
visual continuity, street level, 70

Walt Disney Company, 143–145
Ward, Alan, 3, 9, 11, 85, *127*, 199–200, 201
    "Certainty to Flexibility: Planning and Design
        History," 9, 29–73
Washington, D.C.-area
    as destination for "creative class," 113
    government agencies and contractors, 113
    hotel and office space markets, 89–90
    housing market growth, 111–113
    labor force, 111–113
    retail space market, 87–88
    soaring land values, 114
Washington Post, The, 61
West Market townhouses and condominiums, 14, *20*
    planning for, 94
Westbrook Partners, 97, 104
Wharton Real Estate Review, 71
Whittlesey & Conklin, 35, 37, 40, 41
    early inflexible scheme (1963), *185*
Wilson Sinsini, 100
Wong, Ken, 85
Woodlands, The, 105
Wright, Henry, 33

zoning policies, 18, 67, 82–83,
    eight-mile retail restriction, 87